THE NEEDS OF OTHERS

Human Rights, International
Organizations, and Intervention
in Rwanda, 1994

OTHER TITLES IN THIS SERIES

Also Available

THE NEEDS OF OTHERS

Human Rights, International
Organizations, and Intervention
in Rwanda, 1994

Kelly McFall, Newman University

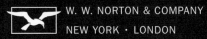
W. W. NORTON & COMPANY
NEW YORK · LONDON

BARNARD
REACTING TO THE PAST

W. W. Norton & Company has been independent since its founding in 1923, when William Warder Norton and Mary D. Herter Norton first published lectures delivered at the People's Institute, the adult education division of New York City's Cooper Union. The firm soon expanded its program beyond the Institute, publishing books by celebrated academics from America and abroad. By midcentury, the two major pillars of Norton's publishing program—trade books and college texts—were firmly established. In the 1950s, the Norton family transferred control of the company to its employees, and today—with a staff of four hundred and a comparable number of trade, college, and professional titles published each year—W. W. Norton & Company stands as the largest and oldest publishing house owned wholly by its employees.

Editor: Justin Cahill
Project Editor: Caitlin Moran
Assistant Editor: Rachel Taylor
Managing Editor, College: Marian Johnson
Production Manager: Stephen Sajdak
Marketing Manager, History: Sarah England Bartley
Design Director: Rubina Yeh
Book Design: Alexandra Charitan
Permissions Manager: Megan Schindel
Composition: Jouve North America
Cartographer: Mapping Specialists, Ltd.
Manufacturing: Sheridan Books

Library of Congress Cataloging-in-Publication Data

Names: McFall, Kelly, author.
Title: The needs of others : human rights, international organizations, and
   intervention in Rwanda, 1994 / Kelly McFall.
Other titles: "Reacting to the past" series.
Description: New York : W. W. Norton & Company, 2019. | Series: Reacting to
   the past | Includes bibliographical references.
Identifiers: LCCN 2018046621 | ISBN 9780393673777 (pbk.)
Subjects: LCSH: Rwanda—History—Civil War, 1994—Atrocities—Problems,
   exercises, etc. | Genocide—Rwanda—History—20th century—Problems,
   exercises, etc. | Humanitarian intervention—Rwanda—History—20th
   century—Problems, exercises, etc. | United Nations—Peacekeeping
   forces—Rwanda—Problems, exercises, etc.
Classification: LCC DT450.435 .M385 2019 | DDC 967.5710431—dc23 LC record available at https://lccn.loc.gov/2018046621

W. W. Norton & Company, Inc., 500 Fifth Avenue, New York, NY 10110
W. W. Norton & Company Ltd., 15 Carlisle Street, London W1D 3BS

2 3 4 5 6 7 8 9 0

ABOUT THE AUTHOR

Kelly McFall is professor of history and Director of the Honors Program at Newman University, where he teaches broadly in modern history and genocide studies. He received his Ph.D. from The Ohio State University. He's been involved with Reacting since 2008 and currently serves on the Editorial Board. As a member of the Board, he has learned from all of the authors whose games he has read and played. He is a co-author of *Changing the Game: Title IX, Gender, and Athletics in American Universities*, a game in development in the Reacting to the Past Series. He is also the host of the podcast *New Books in Genocide Studies*.

CONTENTS

PART 5: CORE TEXTS   76

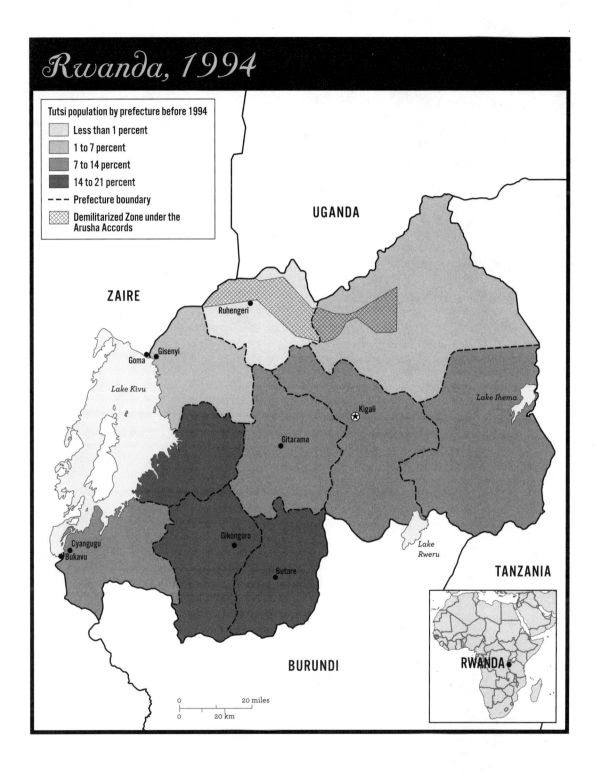

Rwanda, 1994

Tutsi population by prefecture before 1994

- Less than 1 percent
- 1 to 7 percent
- 7 to 14 percent
- 14 to 21 percent
- --- Prefecture boundary
- Demilitarized Zone under the Arusha Accords

UGANDA

ZAIRE

Ruhengeri

Gisenyi

Goma

Lake Kivu

Kigali

Lake Ihema

Gitarama

Cyangugu

Bukavu

Gikongoro

Lake Rweru

Butare

TANZANIA

BURUNDI

0   20 miles
0   20 km

RWANDA

PART 1: INTRODUCTION

BRIEF OVERVIEW OF THE GAME

What responsibility do we have for our fellow human beings? What right do we have to intervene in peoples' lives to prevent them from hurting others? What, in the end, can and should (or must) we do about injustice and oppression? Are we, in fact, our brother's (or sister's) keeper?

These are thorny questions in the abstract, but things become even more complicated when we think specifically about how our governments should respond to real problems facing people across the globe. Despite the many scientific discoveries and economic gains of the past centuries, the world remains a hard place for many. Whether because of lack of resources, regional instability, or governmental oppression, people continue to suffer. It would be wonderful to help everyone, but the painful truth is that governments, like individuals, lack the time, money, and knowledge to do so. We must choose who to help. But how can we choose?

The game *The Needs of Others* asks you to wrestle with these fundamental questions. It does so by immersing you into the world of international policy making and public opinion in April and May of 1994. As the game begins, a long-simmering conflict within Rwanda breaks out into massive violence, and the United Nations (UN) must decide how to respond. Some players will, as part of the UN Security Council (UNSC), have the authority and responsibility to debate proposals and make policy. Others, as leaders of nongovernmental organizations (NGOs), Journalists, or Representatives of Public Opinion, will attempt to learn more about what's going on in Rwanda and influence public policy accordingly. These players will write papers, ask questions, and hold demonstrations to pressure policy makers. All of this takes place in an environment complicated by inadequate information, pressure to make rapid decisions, and outside demands on the time and intellectual energy of policy makers.

The game begins shortly after someone shoots down Rwandan President Juvénal Habyarimana's plane over Kigali in April 1994, which sparks waves of violence. With information arriving to the UN rapidly but haphazardly, you will have to make decisions. Should the UN peacekeeping mission be withdrawn or strengthened? Is the fighting in Rwanda a civil war or something else? Does the UN have an obligation to intervene? If so, how can this be done successfully? Who will pay for it? The UNSC will debate all of these questions and more. You'll need to balance moral beliefs with practical constraints, what you believe is right and what you believe is possible. Presenting your decisions to the public will challenge you even more. In particular, events in Rwanda may overtake debates in New York. But, as always, lives rest on your decisions.

PROLOGUE

"They call this spring?"

You've spent more than five years of your life in New York, but you're still surprised how slowly warmth returns. At home, flowers would be blooming, children swinging on the playground and parents cutting the lawn. You smile wistfully as you pull your hood up over your ears. Spring may be coming to Manhattan. But it's not here yet.

Of course, your being here is almost as unlikely as spring in early April. Growing up in a small town in Georgia, no one expected you to do anything other than wait tables or get pregnant. Most of your friends thought this quite enough. But something about that didn't work for you. Somehow, being born in the South during the civil rights era made you believe your life had to have a purpose.

You found that purpose in serving others. You worked shifts at the homeless shelter and tutored poor children in reading while in college. But what made your heart explode was the unimaginable suffering of the poor in Africa and Asia. So you tried to understand the big picture, majoring in political science and African studies at Emory and getting a master's in public policy from Georgetown. You worked hard, compiling the essential portfolio of references, internships, and writings that would make you competitive in a world so different from that in which you grew up.

You pause and laugh at yourself as you turn onto Fifth Avenue. You've always been a little driven (well, maybe more than a little). Sure, you goofed off some as well. But you've always been in a bit of a hurry. An old boyfriend said once that you were so obsessed about being on time you'd get someplace before you'd decided to go there (must have been hard for him to get along with you. He was never much interested in being prompt). Not a surprise you've arrived for your 12:30 lunch at 12:10. You decide to walk around the block a couple times before you enter the restaurant. At least you'll burn some calories as you wait.

Your passion (self-discipline?) paid off. Just before defending your thesis, you accepted a job with Human Rights Watch (HRW), one of the most prominent non-governmental organizations in the new field of international human rights. There you would research and write about human rights in Africa. How you celebrated that night.

That was a heady time for everyone in the human rights field. Until the late 1980s, the twentieth century had been a period of almost unrelenting pain, despair, and desperation. Two global wars in 30 years had left perhaps 60 million people dead. Along the way, the combatants had ignored or dismissed the rights of non-combatants, exploiting women and children as forced labor, driving populations out of their home-lands, and, notoriously, targeting certain groups for extermination. The ashes of these fires were barely cold, however, when more conflicts broke out. Indeed, a diplomatic struggle between the Soviet Union and the United States smoldered for decades. Jour-nalists called it the "Cold War," but that didn't prevent fighting from erupting in Korea, Vietnam, Afghanistan, and other countries. Those who insisted on the need to oppose communism may have been right. That was small comfort, however, to the victims. Year after year, the rivalry sabotaged the efforts of governments and international organiza-tions to resettle refugees, educate children, and eradicate disease. Authoritarian rulers exploited alliances with one side or the other to enrich themselves, suppress free speech and eliminate their opponents. At its worst, the Cold War enabled or obscured geno-cide in Cambodia, Pakistan, and elsewhere.

But the collapse of the Soviet Union in 1991, just a few years back, seemed to reaf-firm the possibility of change. You remember footage of candlelit marches in Leipzig, thousands upon thousands of people daring the police to fire upon them, demanding the return of their country to its people, chants of "Wir sind das Volk" (We are the people) echoing down the Marktplatz. In Leipzig, as in Berlin, Budapest, Sofia, and Moscow, the police avoided the people's gazes, looking down and refusing to fire. Ordinary people, you learned, can demand their rights be respected.

You look down at your watch. 12:25. Close enough. It will take you a few minutes to get a table anyway. And Ben, the colleague you're meeting for lunch, knows you well. He'll make an effort to be on time.

CNN is on in the background. During a slight lull in the conversation around you, the television seems to grow louder. You glance up. You recognize the familiar images of war-torn Bosnia. Reluctantly, you listen more closely.

". . . without it thousands of people are going to die!" A woman, sounding angry.

"But you can't help people who won't help themselves," a man responds, his tone carefully calculated to sound "rational." You grimace. Since when did caring for others become irrational?

The crawl at the bottom of the screen identifies the program as one of the talk shows popping up everywhere on cable. The network recruits the loudest and angriest speakers, lets them yell at each other for 30 minutes, and calls it news. They don't seem to care very much about informing people anymore. But you know well the power of public opinion. Politicians care about what people are talking about most, not about what matters most.

You laugh self-consciously. So cynical you've become.

When you joined HRW in 1990, people buzzed with optimism. Groups of ordinary people (what political scientists called "civil society") had triumphed over dictatorships. People, and people's fates, mattered again. So, everyone assumed, would the organizations that tried to help them. The roadblocks facing the UN would be removed, non-governmental organizations (NGOs) empowered, and national governments supportive. The new century, while not perfect, would be one of cooperation toward the common goal of human prosperity and dignity.

So you set to work. Assigned to assist Alison Des Forges, a longtime researcher for Human Rights Watch, you quickly came to share her affection and concern for Central Africa. You traveled there twice, once to Uganda and once to Burundi. You wrote reports, lobbied Congress, and tried to interest journalists in the field. You threw yourself into your job.

Unfortunately, dreams rarely come true. Humanitarian NGOs worked extraordinarily hard to address emergencies. But they lacked the resources to resolve conflicts or keep the peace. This left the UN as the 'first responder' in civil wars and governmental collapse. While the number of UN peacekeeping missions to other countries exploded, actually keeping the peace proved surprisingly difficult. The UN lacked both the resources and the support of national governments to plan, staff, and execute peacekeeping missions effectively. A small and increasingly overburdened UN staff tried desperately to meet competing demands on its time and attention. With too many balls in the air, its actions were frequently too little, too late. Moreover, national and international politics continued to obstruct humanitarian efforts even after the end of the Cold War. In South Ossetia, Iraq, Sierra Leone, and elsewhere, global peace concealed local tragedies.

"Even if we tried to help, what could we do?" The patient-sounding man again, explaining to the world why suffering people could not be rescued. "Air power won't be enough. To stop ethnic cleansing you need boots on the ground. And what country is going to send troops to Bosnia? The place is almost Third World. Rural, poverty-ridden, divided by ancient ethnic tensions. . . ."

You wince. *Ethnic tensions.* Code words for "tribal wars." If he had been talking about Africa, he wouldn't have pulled his punches. On the other hand, what was the chance that Africa would get even five minutes on this show . . .?

It had all blown up in Africa. Just last year in Somalia a UN force tried to enforce its mandate by seizing the leader of one of the warring factions. The operation went wrong, and Somali militiamen killed 18 American soldiers. Teenagers dragged one of the bodies through the streets in front of cheering Somali crowds and shocked journalists. The failure, shown over and over again on television throughout the world, severely damaged the credibility of the UN in general and of peace making in particular. Politicians quickly learned the only news about Africa that mattered was news of American deaths.

". . . you believe we have a moral obligation to help those in need?" The female guest, looking deflated. Her tone makes it clear you missed the plaintive "*don't*" at the beginning of her sentence.

"Of course. But first and foremost we have an obligation to our own people. Let's face it. Bosnia is a quagmire. What was the lesson we all learned from Mogadishu? Never again send our boys into a place where you can't tell the good guys from the bad. Never again ask them to die to enforce an unwanted peace."

You smile sourly. Never again. So many people had solemnly pledged "never again" as they exited the recent movie *Schindler's List*. What has the world learned, when the camps holding Bosnian prisoners at Omarska and Keraterm look so much like those at the Nazi camps of Dachau and Buchenwald?

Where was Ben, anyway? You glance up at the clock again. Now you're worried for a different reason. It's not like him to be quite so late.

"You have to recognize that, in the end, it's not in our national interest to send troops to Bosnia."

Ah. The mask is off.

The woman sputtered. "Why does it all come down to national interest? What about the common good?"

"Because, in the end, governments exist to defend their own people, not others. We live in the world we have, not the world we wish for."

Isn't that the truth? No one anymore thinks we can change the world. Still, it's the hope that you can make a difference, even a small one, which keeps you going every day.

You glance up at the television, wondering how the woman will react. Something in the crawl catches your attention. "The plane carrying Presidents Habyarimana of Rwanda and Ntaryamira of Burundi was shot down today as it approached the airport in Kigali."

Shit. That's why Ben didn't show up. And why you won't be eating lunch, at least not here. Who knows what's going to happen in Rwanda now. Only one thing is certain. It won't be good.

You grab your purse and throw down a ten for the bartender. It's going to be a long day.

WHAT IS REACTING TO THE PAST?

Reacting to the Past is a series of historical role-playing games. Students are given detailed game books that place them in moments of historical controversy and intellectual ferment. The class becomes a public body of some sort; students, in role, become particular individuals from the period, often as members of a faction. Their purpose is to advance a policy agenda and achieve their victory objectives. To do so, they will undertake research and write speeches and position papers, and they will also give formal speeches, participate in informal debates and negotiations, and otherwise work to win the game. After a few preparatory lectures, the game begins and the players are in charge; the instructor serves as adviser or "Gamemaster" (GM). Outcomes sometimes differ from the actual history; a postmortem session at the end of the game sets the record straight.

The following is an outline of what you will encounter in Reacting and what you will be expected to do. While these elements are typical of every Reacting game, it is important to remember that each game has its own special quirks.

HOW TO REACT

Game Setup

Your instructor will spend some time before the beginning of the game helping you understand the historical background. During the setup period, you will read several different kinds of materials:

- The game book (from which you are reading now), which includes historical information, rules and elements of the game, and essential documents.

- Your role sheet, which includes a short biography of the historical person you will model in the game as well as that person's ideology, objectives, responsibilities, and resources. Your role may be an actual figure or a composite.

In addition to the game book, you may also be required to read primary and secondary sources (perhaps including one or more accompanying books), which provide further information and arguments for use during the game. Often you will be expected to conduct research to bolster your papers and speeches.

Read all of this contextual material and all of these documents and sources before the game begins. And just as important, go back and reread these materials throughout the game. A second reading while *in role* will deepen your understanding and alter your perspective because ideas take on a different aspect when seen through the eyes of a partisan actor.

Players who have carefully read the materials and who know the rules of the game will invariably do better than those who rely on general impressions and uncertain recollections.

Game Play

Once the game begins, class sessions are presided over by students. In most cases, a single student serves as a kind of presiding officer. The instructor then becomes the Gamemaster and takes a seat in the back of the room. Though he or she will not lead the class sessions, the GM may do any of the following:

- Pass notes

- Announce important events, some of which may be the result of student actions; others are instigated by the GM

- Redirect proceedings that have gone off track

The presiding officer is expected to observe basic standards of fairness, but as a fail-safe device, most Reacting to the Past games employ the "Podium Rule," which allows a student who has not been recognized to approach the podium and wait for a chance to speak. Once at the podium, the student has the floor and must be heard.

Role sheets contain private, secret information, which students are expected to guard. You are advised, therefore, to exercise caution when discussing your role with others. Your role sheet probably identifies likely allies, but even they may not always be trustworthy. However, keeping your own counsel, or saying nothing to anyone, is not an option. To achieve your objectives, you must speak with others. You will never muster the voting strength to prevail without allies. Collaboration and coalition building are at the heart of every game.

These discussions must lead to action, which often means proposing, debating, and passing legislation. Someone therefore must be responsible for introducing the measure and explaining its particulars. And always remember that a Reacting game is only a game— resistance, attack, and betrayal are not to be taken personally, since game opponents are merely acting as their roles direct.

Some games feature strong alliances called *factions*; these are tight-knit groups with fixed objectives. Games with factions all include roles called Indeterminates or independents. They operate outside of the established factions. They are not all entirely neutral; some are biased on certain issues. If you are in a faction, cultivating these players is in your interest, because they can be convinced to support your position. If you are lucky enough to have drawn one of the roles of an Indeterminate you should be pleased; you will likely play a pivotal role in the outcome of the game.

Game Requirements

Students in Reacting games practice persuasive writing, public speaking, critical thinking, teamwork, negotiation, problem solving, collaboration, adapting to changing circumstances, and working under pressure to meet deadlines. Your instructor will explain the specific requirements for your class. In general, though, a Reacting game asks you to perform three distinct activities:

Reading and Writing. This standard academic work is carried on more purposefully in a Reacting course, because what you read is put to immediate use and what you write is meant to persuade others to act the way you want them to. The reading load may have slight variations from role to role; the writing requirement depends on your particular course. Papers are often policy statements, but they can also be autobiographies, battle plans, spy reports, newspapers, poems, or after-game reflections. Papers provide the foundation for the speeches delivered in class.

Public Speaking and Debate. In the course of a game, almost everyone is expected to deliver at least one formal speech from the podium (the length of the game and the size of the class will determine the number of speeches). Debate follows. Debate can be impromptu, raucous, and fast-paced and results in decisions voted on by the body. Gamemasters may stipulate that students must deliver their papers from memory when at the podium or may insist that students wean themselves from dependency on written notes as the game progresses.

Wherever the game imaginatively puts you, it will surely not put you in the classroom of a twenty-first-century American college. Accordingly, the colloquialisms and familiarities of today's college life are out of place. Never open your speech with a salutation like "Hi guys" when something like "Fellow citizens!" would be more appropriate.

Never be friendless when standing at the podium. Do your best to have at least one supporter second your proposal, come to your defense, or admonish inattentive members of the body. Note passing and side conversations, while common occurrences, will likely spoil the effect of your speech; so you and your supporters should insist on order before such behavior becomes too disruptive. Ask the presiding officer to assist you, if necessary, and the Gamemaster as a last resort.

Strategizing. Communication among students is an essential feature of Reacting games. You will find yourself writing emails, texting, attending out-of-class meetings, or gathering for meals on a fairly regular basis. The purpose of frequent communication is to lay out a strategy for advancing your agenda and thwarting the agenda of your opponents and to hatch plots to ensnare individuals troubling to your cause. When communicating with a fellow student in or out of class, always assume that he or she is speaking to you in role. If you want to talk about the "real world," make that clear.

Counterfactuals

The game seeks to plunge you into the debates and discussions of the spring of 1994. However, to ensure playability and to guarantee the emergence of certain intellectually important issues, the game alters specific elements of the historical past. They include the following:

- **UN ambassadors have more autonomy and power than is historically accurate.** Ambassadors in the game are not allowed to stall by pleading the need to consult with their president/prime minister/king (note: consulting with the ambassador's home government about the possibility of providing military support is not considered stalling). However, in all cases, players' role sheets reflect the priorities of their national leadership and should compel them to act in historically reasonable ways.

- **Limitations on the number of private sessions the UNSC may hold.** In real life, the UNSC can guarantee private deliberations by calling almost unlimited informal or executive sessions. In fact, the UNSC conducts all business in private session, convening public sessions only to hold formal votes. However, in the game, private sessions would prevent many players from listening to important debates, and would exclude them from the classroom for significant amounts of time. Accordingly, the UNSC is allowed to call *only two* private sessions of twenty minutes each during the course of the game. Naturally, players may meet privately *outside* of class time as much as they like. How private these meetings remain depends on the participants.

- **Rwanda replaced by Indonesia on the UNSC.** In real life, Rwanda was a member of the UNSC during the period re-created by the game. I have chosen not to ask a student to play this role for reasons that should become apparent during the game. To bring the UNSC up to its standard fifteen countries, I've added Indonesia, which did not have a place on the Security Council in 1994.

- **Not fully representational of a complex reality.** To emphasize specific issues in the game and because relatively little is known about some of the smaller countries in the UNSC during 1994, I have crafted perspectives and victory conditions that would logically fit these roles. Although I have tried to craft roles that match the historical behavior of the countries represented in the game, one should not assume each named ambassador held exactly the views presented in the role sheets.

 PART 2: HISTORICAL BACKGROUND

CHRONOLOGY

The following timeline is designed specifically to fit this game. Thus it privileges certain events over others. In particular, it gives greater weight to European influence than would a broader chronology. In addition, it omits items that are unknown to some players. In other words, every player would know all the events listed in this chronology. But you should not assume it is complete, especially as it nears 1994. It's your responsibility to discover what has been left out.

1650s   Ruganzu Ndori founds the Nyiginya kingdom in the center of modern-day Rwanda.
- This region is often referred to as the Nduga.

1780s   The Nyiginya kingdom begins a process of gradual expansion that will, over the course of a century, make it the preeminent polity in Rwanda.

1800s   Popular beliefs about what it means to be Hutu and Tutsi change and solidify in response to a series of political, economic, and administrative changes.

1880s   First European explorers arrive in Rwanda.

1899   Germany declares Rwanda a German colony.

1919   In the aftermath of the Treaty of Versailles, the League of Nations gives Belgium the mandate to rule over Rwanda.

1930s   Belgium issues identification cards, conducts research on the racial makeup of Rwandans, and introduces a variety of other policies that contribute to a racialization of Hutu and Tutsi identities.

1959-62   Belgium bends to Rwandan pressure and grants Rwanda independence.
- During the violence, tens of thousands of Tutsis flee to surrounding countries.

1962-67   Armed invasion by Tutsi refugees is repelled by the Rwandan armed forces.
- Pogroms against Tutsis occur sporadically during the violence.
- Racial violence kills perhaps a thousand Tutsis, and thousands of others leave the country.
- Violence continues, at lessor or greater intensity, through 1967.

1973   Juvénal Habyarimana overthrows President Grégoire Kayibanda in an armed coup and becomes president.

1978   A new constitution ratified in this year makes the National Republican Movement for Democracy and Development (MRND) Party the only legal political party in Rwanda.

mid-1980s	The prices of coffee and other Rwandan exports drop precipitously, leading to financial and economic difficulties.
1988	Rwandan Patriotic Front (RPF) is founded.
1989	The end of the Cold War accelerates Western calls for the introduction of multiparty democracy and liberal economic reforms in Rwanda.
1990	• **October:** The RPF invades Rwanda from Uganda. • **November:** President Habyarimana announces the legalization of other political parties.
1992	Opening of negotiations in Arusha between the RPF and the Rwandan government. • In the wake of increasing tension, major political parties organize party militias.
1993	• **July:** Radio Télévision Libre des Mille Collines (RTLM) begins broadcasting. • **August:** Arusha accords signed. • **October:** UNSC approves the formation of UN Assistance Mission for Rwanda (UNAMIR). • A military coup in neighboring Burundi kills the Hutu president Ndadaye and leads to massive racial violence. • Tens of thousands of Hutus killed and hundreds of thousands flee to Rwanda
April 6, 1994	President Habyarimana's plane is shot down while approaching Kigali airport.

A SHORT HISTORY OF RWANDA

Questions to consider while reading the historical background: What impact did Belgian rule have on Rwanda? Define what it means to be a Hutu and a Tutsi. How this meaning has changed over time? How have Hutus and Tutsis interacted politically over time? How and why did the stability of Rwanda under Habyarimana decay and why is that important for Rwandan history? What role did Burundi and Uganda play in the history of Rwanda from 1961 to 1993? Why did world leaders decide an international organization was necessary in the aftermath World War I? Why did this fail? Why try again after World War II? What were some of the ways that the Cold War impacted the shape and actions of the UN? How did the end of the Cold War change UN attitudes and behaviors? How did events in Somalia change UN perspectives on humanitarian intervention? Why? How and why did the UN get involved in Rwanda? What was its mission there? How did it try to achieve it?

By **colonialism**, I mean the period during which European countries claimed and exerted political and administrative control over African (and Asian) countries. Although this happened at different times in different places, for most of Africa it began roughly around 1885 and concluded between 1960 and 1980. The nature of this political and administrative control varied widely across Africa, and it is accordingly dangerous to generalize the African experience during these years. I use the term *postcolonial* instead of "independent" because the latter implies Rwanda was somehow not independent before the arrival of Europeans.

To understand modern Rwanda, you can imagine its history as being roughly divided into three parts: precolonial, colonial and postcolonial. Already, I've vastly oversimplified, and we need to remember the region experienced important changes and developments during each phase. But, for our purposes, it's a useful simplification. Each period saw the emergence of a distinctive set of political institutions and networks of authority. In each period, the dominant culture shifted, and new economic and social institutions emerged. And during each period, the Rwandan people had a distinctive understanding of their own history. Indeed, neither colonial nor postcolonial Rwanda could escape the influence of the past. Rather, modern-day Rwanda is a distinctive mix of all three. Each period must be understood to understand Rwanda's present.

Precolonial History

For centuries, geography divided the area we now call Rwanda into dozens of small independent regions, occupied by **lineages** that presided over territories and economic resources. These lineages controlled one, or a few or occasionally more than a few, of the proverbial thousand hills that run through much of Rwanda. To make things easy, we'll call these *states*, although the term is not exactly correct. The relative power and success of these states changed over time. But the nature of the social system in the region stayed stable for a long period of time.

The people who lived in the region were largely similar. They thought of themselves as members of lineages, of clans (loosely described as sets of lineages),

Lineage: A group of individuals who can trace their ancestry through their fathers to a common ancestor. In Rwanda, these lineages often go back three to six generations. This family relationship was and remains critical in everyday life and in politics.

In 1994, Hutus made up about 85 percent of the population of Rwanda, the Tutsi about 15 percent. These figures are probably pretty accurate for the earlier period as well. A third group, the Twa, numbered only about 1 percent of the population and plays little role in the events of this game.

as men and women, as farmers and herders, and as Hutus and Tutsis. The meanings of the words *Hutu* and *Tutsi* are slippery, because they changed significantly over time. At one time the word *Hutu* was simply a derogatory label, used to insult or diminish someone. The word *Tutsi* went through a variety of different transformations, referring at one point to a small subset of herders, at another meaning "combatant." Over time, these labels came to refer to occupation, with herders labeled Tutsi and farmers labeled Hutu.[1]

Well over half of the Rwandan population in the 1700s and 1800s was Hutu, while the Tutsis were a small but significant minority. There was and is a "typical" set of physical characteristics for each group. The Tutsis tend to be taller and thinner and are lighter colored. The Hutus, in contrast, are often shorter, more thickly built, and darker. However, these statements are generalizations, largely accurate in the aggregate, but only sometimes on the individual level. Hutus and Tutsis have often married each other and the originally typical physical characteristics (even then difficult to distinguish) have become almost impossible to apply in the real world. There were and are tall Hutus, short Tutsis, and everything in between.

Social scientists often distinguish between the terms *race* and *ethnicity*. **Ethnicity**, they argue, is a kind of identity based on shared cultural characteristics— language, traditions, beliefs, and so on. **Race** is defined by shared physical characteristics that people consider culturally significant. These are problematic terms and should not be used carelessly. For considerations of space, I'll use *race* when referring to Rwanda and *ethnicity* (or ethnic groups) in places like Bosnia, where contemporaries used that word. In all cases, remember these are constructed identities, not biological ones.

Most important here is to recognize that Hutu and Tutsi in this early period were something like social categories, not racial ones. Which category you belonged to was never a mystery. But your answer might change over time. Your children might, by dint of hard work or sheer good fortune (or, alternately, bad luck), earn the right to give a different answer. To use academic language, one's place in society was not predetermined by the category one belonged to, nor was one fated to remain in that category forever. That doesn't mean the categories didn't exist. It just meant that this was only one part of your identity.

Beginning in the 1700s, a small state in the center of present-day Rwanda, in a region called Nduga, began a 200-year process of expansion. This Nyiginya kingdom first exerted its control over the central hill country, then the eastern lowlands, and finally, after much fighting, over the western highlands. Rarely did this expansion represent the execution of a long-term strategy. Rather, it represented the cumulative impact of dozens of individual decisions. But collectively these individual decisions resulted in the growth of Nduga influence and authority. By the end of the nineteenth century, the monarch of this region *claimed* control over most of modern Rwanda.

Claiming control did not make it true. Influential lineages at court challenged the power of the king throughout the century. Away from the court, the kingdom was less a coherent territory than it was a set of alliances, with Nduga influence strong in regions close to the center and weak in regions farther away.

Late in the nineteenth century and into the twentieth, the Nyiginya kings moved to strengthen their control and influence at the court and in the recently acquired territories. In doing so, they retained and strengthened systems that could amplify their power and introduced new ones that increased personal and communal responsibilities to the government. For example, they created new administrative positions and staffed them with men loyal to the court. They harnessed traditions that required village members to spend time working for the community and required men to work on projects for local or regional governments. Critically, only Hutus were required to do this, not Tutsis. Finally (at least for our purposes), the kings attempted to eliminate the infighting in the court and strengthen the personal authority of their family and lineage. These were important and long-lasting changes. But they were incomplete. The political leaders in the center made them exactly to limit the freedom and authority of others. It shouldn't surprise us that these "others" resisted as much as possible. This resistance would continue into the twentieth century and influence the way the king responded to the arrival of Europeans.

The effort to centralize power and control had other consequences. Most important, it began a critical change in Rwandans' self-understanding. For the changes worked almost universally in favor of Tutsis and against the interests of the Hutus. Government officials overwhelmingly selected Tutsis to occupy the new offices centralization required. In addition, the expansion and intensification of the system of obligatory communal labor and other changes in how taxes were levied and collected hurt Hutu regions and lineages significantly more than those of the Tutsi.

Favoring Tutsis was not accidental—it was a deliberate strategy to weaken peripheral leaders. It had predictable consequences. The local leaders resisted the imposition of new burdens on them—sometimes politically, sometimes militarily. More important in the long term, imposing political rights and burdens based on identity changed the nature of that identity itself. Quite quickly, the categories of Hutu and Tutsi changed from social and malleable to political and fixed. Jan Vansina puts it best: "From this point on, 'Hutu' and 'Tutsi' would no longer designate a relative category with respect to class or dependency or occupation, but become an absolute one."[2] Some present-day historians would question the definitiveness of Vansina's claim. But most would agree that the process of solidifying the nature of Hutu and Tutsi accelerated greatly during this period.

In sum, one way of thinking about the period from 1700 to 1900 in Rwanda is to see it as an attempt (a successful one) by one group in Rwandan society to win power and influence over the others. The political conflicts and economic and administrative changes that resulted from this dominated Rwandan society in the nineteenth and early twentieth centuries. But the importance of these conflicts was not limited to who was in charge. They shaped how people answered the question of who they were. And they did so in ways that were divisive, leading Hutus to resent Tutsi dominance and Tutsis to feel themselves superior to Hutus.

Rwanda under the Europeans

When European colonialists arrived as part of the great wave of European expansion in the late nineteenth century, they found a complex and rapidly changing situation. To maximize the benefits and minimize the costs of their control over Rwanda, they would rule in a way that intensified the changes already under way. They would do so in cooperation with the Tutsi royal court, who would see Belgian hopes as a pathway to achieving its own goals. The ensuring reforms would set the stage for the racial conflicts and political clashes of the second half of the twentieth century.

German Rule and Legacies of European Racial Thinking In 1884, European nations with overseas interests gathered together in Berlin. These countries were racing to seize control of African territory, and diplomats hoped to avoid the chance of accidental conflict between European nations by carving up the African continent. This conference assigned Germany a vast area of East Central Africa, including modern-day Tanzania, Burundi, and Rwanda. Ironically, in 1884, no German had set foot in Rwanda. This would remain true until 1894, when the German explorer Gustav Adolf von Götzen entered the country. The Germans quickly negotiated an agreement with the Rwandan king, acknowledging Germany's formal authority over Rwanda. However, they made little effort to exert control on the ground and largely left their Rwandan subjects to their own devices. In the end, German colonial control had little impact on Rwanda.

German control would end during World War I (1914–18), when Belgian forces seized Rwanda from the Germans. The Treaty of Versailles that ended the war—marking Germany's defeat—ratified this change, assigning control of Rwanda to Belgium. This would be critical to Rwandan history, for Belgium would not be nearly as hands-off a colonial ruler as Germany had been. The Belgians saw the colonies as a valuable material and diplomatic resource. To extract this value, they wanted a colony that was both stable and productive. To do this, they needed an ally. And elite Tutsis leaders, who believed themselves the rightful leaders of Rwanda due to their historical connection to the Rwandan monarchy, were willing to cooperate.

The ideas of the Catholic Church and of earlier European explorers shaped European perceptions of African peoples as inferior as well as the policies colonial administrators would draw from these perceptions. Missionaries who arrived in the region in the late nineteenth century had immediately applied racial thinking and the ideas of **Social Darwinism** to their approach in dealing with peoples of Central Africa. In short, they believed the different groups they encountered were fundamentally—biologically—different. For example, Father Léon Classe, a French missionary later appointed bishop of Rwanda, proclaimed in 1902 that the Tutsis were "superb humans" who displayed both Aryan and Semitic characteristics. Another priest, the Belgian Father François Menard, characterized Tutsis as "European(s) under a black skin." Catholic officials repeated these ideas time after time in the early decades of the twentieth century and in so doing taught Belgians in Europe and in Africa how to understand Rwanda.[3]

Social Darwinism: A belief, popular in the late nineteenth and early twentieth centuries, that the principles of natural selection, developed by Charles Darwin to describe the biological evolution of species, also applied within the human species to explain physical and sociological differences. Adherents believed humans were divided into races, which competed with each other for limited resources and survival in a dangerous natural world. The underlying assumption was that some races were better than others, an idea that validated European claims that, as a "superior race," their countries deserved to rule over "inferior" peoples.

European explorers and writers brought similar ideas. Most famously, they referred to a biblical story about Noah and his sons to reinforce their supposedly scientific explanation for Tutsi superiority. Drawn from the book of Genesis, the story recounts a drunken Noah laying naked on the floor. His son Ham sees him and neglects to show respect by covering him up (some interpreters argue that this is veiled language and the text implies that Ham raped Noah). Ham's brothers, in contrast, covered Noah and cared for him. As a consequence, when Noah awoke, he cursed Ham's son Canaan to be the servant (or slave, in some translations) of Ham's brothers Shem and Japheth. Europeans interpreted this story in a variety of ways to understand the place of Africa and Africans in the world. Here, we need only consider its relevance to Rwanda. In this account, the descendants of Ham moved south to Africa. As they did so, they—a cursed people, to be sure, but still Western—brought civilization to the Africans. In particular, the Tutsis, a so-called Hamitic people originally living in Ethiopia, moved to Rwanda and civilized the regions' African natives, the Hutus and the Twas. Initially articulated by English explorer John Speke in 1864, the explanation quickly became popular. Already by 1870, Catholic leaders gathered at the Vatican I conference called on Europeans to save the "hapless Hamites caught amidst Negros."[4]

Belgian Rule and the Tutsi Court When Belgian officials formally assumed control of Rwanda after the Treaty of Versailles, they imagined the future of their new colony through the lens of these racial and religious assumptions. Their goal was simple: to maximize the benefit to Belgium while empowering the Church to convert Rwandans to Christianity. They would do this by relying on the royal Tutsi leadership to implement Belgian policies. As they did so, these same policies would also benefit the Tutsis. By doing so, these policies would reinforce (or, put differently, create) the racial differences that the Belgians believed inherent in nature (but had in reality begun to harden in the 1800s). The story of the 1920s and 1930s, then, was the story of reform after reform that both relied on and privileged the Tutsi minority.

This is not, however, a story of powerful Europeans exploiting powerless Africans (or of cynical Europeans exploiting naive Africans). Rather, the Tutsi court chose to partner with the Belgians on those occasions, albeit for their own ends. As you'll recall, the extension of Nduga control over most of modern-day Rwanda was relatively recent and incomplete. Contests over power and authority continued in many of the outlying regions. Accordingly, the royal court saw the Belgian presence as a convenient way to expand its own influence. The result was what Catharine Newbury, one of the most important historians of Rwanda, described as "dual colonialism," a process by which Belgium colonized Rwanda and the core Nduga region simultaneously extended its control over areas until then not fully assimilated.[5]

This is not to say that this partnership was always smooth. In particular, Belgians in Rwanda were wary of the power and influence of the existing mwami. Accordingly, they worked to decentralize power to the regional and local chiefs. Indeed in 1931, when the current king, Mwami Musinga, refused to go along with Belgian desires, they deposed and replaced him with his son, Charles Mutara III Rudahigwa. That they ignored long-established Rwandan custom in selecting his son reminds us that, when Belgium wanted to exert control, it could. However, for the most part the colonial rulers cooperated with the existing notables in Rwanda.[6]

Reforms in local government were one aspect of this effort. The Belgians restructured local government to eliminate positions typically occupied by Hutus. In addition, in areas where Hutus remained powerful, the Belgians imported Tutsis from other regions of the country to assume local leadership. As a consequence, Tutsis acquired a virtual monopoly on leadership. By 1959, the last year of uncontested Belgian control over Rwanda, 43 of 45 chiefs were Tutsi as well as 549 out of 559 subchiefs.

Moreover, Belgian leaders and their royal Tutsi allies restructured obligations between superiors and inferiors. These relationships had taken many forms over time, but had ordinarily involved some kind of reciprocal obligations between citizens and leaders. The Belgians built on reforms initiated in the nineteenth century to implement forced labor requirements (but only for Hutus), alter taxation, redistribute land, and dictate where crops would be planted. It is important to remember that these changes were meant primarily to benefit Belgium. But they were implemented by the now overwhelmingly Tutsi-dominated government administration. The result was unsurprising, to say the least: Hutus, in essence, bore the brunt of Belgian attempts to exploit Rwanda's resources, sometimes spending 60 percent of their working lives laboring for the government.

The educational system that emerged in the 1920s and 1930s similarly privileged Tutsis. The Catholic Church had opened schools as early as 1907 to offer Rwandans, particularly Tutsi children, a Western education. The missionary leadership quickly formulated a policy by which these schools would focus on providing Tutsis, whom they considered the born leaders of Rwanda, an education that would allow them to partner with the Belgians in the colonial project of Westernization and progress. In the 1930s, the Church took over responsibility for the entire Rwandan school system from the government. The system that emerged had two tracks. Tutsis were taught in French and prepared for administrative positions. They were told that they would be citizens, even if at the lowest level.

TIP

The question of whether Hutus and Tutsis are racial groups or not will be critical. Read this section carefully.

In contrast, Hutus were taught in Swahili (an African language, thus considered inferior), prepared for manual labor, and taught that, as Africans, they did not deserve citizenship.

Colonial Legacies for Hutus and Tutsis The Belgian–Tutsi partnership and its effects on Rwandan society further cemented the process of making Hutu and Tutsi rigid categories. In particular, Belgians introduced a language of scientific racism that justified and amplified the distinctions between the two groups. While a few Belgians and Rwandans recognized the ambiguous nature of the labels *Hutu* and *Tutsi*, many more convinced themselves and others that these categories were racial and unalterable. They did this by reimagining the precolonial past and inscribing onto institutions and histories a narrative in which the Tutsis were powerful and dignified and the Hutus weak and unsophisticated. For instance, Tutsi leaders and intellectuals began to portray the precolonial social structure as feudal, with the Tutsis playing the part of the nobles and the Hutus being the peasants. In a world newly influenced by Europeans, labeling someone a peasant was to describe them as simple, uneducated, and powerless, while to be a noble was to be honorable, intelligent, and powerful. Suddenly identity in Rwanda was not so fluid: Hutu and Tutsi were becoming powerful markers of identity and status.

Administrative measures reinforced these intellectual trends. The 1933–34 census forced Rwandans to select a racial identity. After this, the government issued identity cards using the census results. These cards, which Rwandans had to carry with them wherever they went, now included race identity, rendering a once-fluid category now unalterable precisely because it was recorded on governmental documents. The result was a country in which racial identity became core to how most Rwandans saw themselves. Most Tutsis, regardless of class, thought of themselves as superior while most Hutus saw themselves as weak and oppressed. Unsurprisingly, publicly expressed hatred of Tutsis by Hutus began to appear.

It's worth pausing a moment to consider the role of the Church. Theologically, Christianity is a universalistic faith, seeing all as brothers and sisters in Christ. This might have led the Catholic Church, which had arrived in Rwanda with the Belgians, to oppose the growth of a racial worldview. However, political and economic ambition rather than religious belief drove conversion to Catholicism. As it became clear the Belgians preferred Christians for governmental positions, masses of Rwandans up to and including the king quickly converted. The Church thus became an extremely influential institution in Rwanda. It ran virtually the entire educational system, where limitations on Hutu access to public goods steered many Hutus to Catholic schools and then the Catholic priesthood. It also played a significant role in creating a moralistic culture, and served as the social glue tying Rwanda together. But few religious leaders, Belgian or indigenous, emphasized the universalist ideas underlying Christian faith. One result was that, while Christian practices were pervasive in Rwanda, ideas of Christian brotherhood played little role in a society increasingly divided by race.[7]

By the 1950s, the essential character of colonial Rwanda was set. Rwanda had completed its transition, begun under the monarchy and encouraged by the Belgians, to a bureaucratic, Christian, racially divided state. It was precisely at this point that the movement for independence began. Rwanda's struggle for independence would be mercifully quick. In the aftermath of independence, however, the country would face the persistent patterns of the past. While the people of Rwanda reshaped and reimaged these patterns, they never escaped them. Nevertheless, Rwandans, like people everywhere, were not prisoners of their past. Their history constrained their choices; it didn't determine them.

Postcolonial Rwanda, 1962–1990

The 1950s and 1960s represented a dramatic turning point in global history. World War II left Belgium, the United Kingdom, France, and the Netherlands, the traditional colonial powers of Europe, severely damaged. The United States, on the other hand, emerged from the war in an unprecedented position, one of two global superpowers and, until the Soviet Union recovered from its own wartime destruction, the clear favorite. Notably, American politicians consistently opposed continued European control over their colonies.

It's not surprising then, that the 1950s and 1960s were the decades of decolonization, a period when previously colonized nations asserted their independence. European powers resisted, seeing their colonies as economic resources and badges of power. In some cases, their efforts led to years of fighting and destruction (as in French Algeria, for example). But for the most part, the need to concentrate on rebuilding Europe after the devastation of the war, combined with American pressure to decolonize, led Europeans to turn away from their African colonies. This happened, too, in Rwanda.

Pressures for decolonization mounted within Rwanda as well. Limited opportunities in education, government administration, and business led to the emergence of a Hutu movement demanding independence. By the 1950s a nascent Hutu civil society had emerged, led by Rwandans including Grégoire Kayibanda, who had attended seminary, taught at a primary school, and then edited a major Catholic newspaper with a Rwandan readership. Quickly, this movement began to demand decolonization. These demands began with independence, but did not end with it. The new Rwanda envisioned by Kayibanda and others would be one where Hutus would finally be in control of their own country. In this new country, then, Hutus would at least enjoy equality of opportunity and, perhaps, much more.

Tutsis responded to calls for independence in different ways. Some Rwandan Tutsis were perfectly content with the status quo, whether because it suited their interests or because they were too busy to care. Others worked with Hutus in envisioning an independent Rwanda where Hutus and Tutsis could work together toward a prosperous future. Still others, often members of the political and economic elite, supported independence, but did so only to ensure the continuation of Tutsi control over the country.

Achieving independence took several years. Pressures for decolonization sparked movement in 1958 after a Hutu politician was assaulted by Tutsi youths. Hutu protests broke out, which in turn sparked a spiral of escalating violence between Hutus and Tutsis, eventually leading Belgium to step in. It was surprising that Belgian leaders supported the idea of independence; even more surprising was their support of Hutus. In particular, younger priests and other Belgian religious figures had begun to lobby their government to free Rwanda. These leaders had lived through the racism and oppression of World War II and now brought these issues to the attention of the colonial government. Persuaded, the Belgian-controlled government significantly increased the role of Hutus in government. Almost simultaneously, they announced elections that, when held, returned an overwhelming number of votes for Hutus. Thus as Belgium announced its intention to offer Rwanda independence in 1961 and formally withdrew in 1962, internal politics favored the Hutus.

The politics and rhetoric of this revolution both revealed perceptions of the past and shaped the future of Rwanda. Speeches made by Tutsi leaders sometimes framed the conflict as between Belgians and Rwandans, intentionally ignoring the racial differences that had come to divide Rwandans. By stressing the conflict as between Rwanda and Belgium, these speeches implicitly dismissed the idea that any real redistribution of power or resources among racial groups was necessary. Hutu rhetoric, in contrast, often highlighted racial divisions and demanded a double revolution: one against the Belgians and another against their allies, the Tutsi leadership.

We can see this difference of rhetoric best through a single example, the Bahutu Manifesto of 1957. In this document, a group of Hutu intellectuals described Rwanda as a "political monopoly" held by Tutsis, who also held "economic, social and cultural" monopolies. The manifesto went on to acknowledge that Tutsis should play a role in an independent Rwanda, but one proportional to the size of their population. The logical conclusion would be a radical expansion of opportunities for Hutus.[8] Accordingly, the Bahutu Manifesto was as much a political document as a rhetorical statement of belief about what the future of Rwanda would look like. The signatories chose their words strategically to help them achieve a political end. In this sense, it was a direct response to the racially neutral rhetoric of many Tutsi elites, which itself downplayed race to preserve its own power. In this way, the revolution not only changed the political facts of who held power—it further encouraged people to see Rwanda through a racial lens. As we'll see, this pattern would continue for decades to come.

In 1962 a coalition government led by Kayibanda and staffed largely by Hutus took control of Rwanda. Now in power, these Rwandan leaders faced a new set of problems, to figure out what this newly independent state should look like. In the immediate aftermath of independence, the political dynamics of Rwanda were complicated. Inside the country, many Hutus hoped to use independence to reverse the historical fact of Tutsi dominance and assume the same kind of dominance the Tutsis had possessed. At the same time, there were some, both Hutus and Tutsis, who imagined a Rwanda where both groups could participate fully. Which side might have won out in the absence of external pressure is hard to say.

The reality, however, was that many Tutsi notables fled the country during the fight for independence, meaning that external affairs would play a large role in determining the shape of the newly independent country. Many refugees were determined to return, to regain their power, and to re-create the power structures of colonial-era Rwanda. Small groups of these refugees, calling themselves *inyenzi* (cockroaches) to signify their persistence, began to launch raids into Rwanda. Over the next two years talk of invading the country to retake their rightful place became common (although the rhetoric concealed significant rifts between various refugee groups). There were not many of these raids—perhaps a dozen or fewer—and they rarely threatened the government directly. But they led to a spiral of racial violence. Raids led to repression of Tutsis within Rwanda, which led more Tutsis to flee, which led to more raids and so on. The most important of these raids came in 1963 when Tutsi refugees came close to taking Kigali, the capital. It was a desperate roll of the dice by a Tutsi faction that was losing the political debate outside of Rwanda. It was not seen that way within the country, however. Motivated both by fear and by political opportunism, the Kayibanda government led a campaign of violence and destruction against Tutsis still living in Rwanda. This campaign lasted several months and killed anywhere from 5,000 to 20,000 Tutsis.[9] In its wake, tens of thousands of elite Tutsis fled their homeland. Estimates vary, but it's reasonable to say that by 1967, when the last of these raids occurred, perhaps 200,000 Tutsi refugees lived in Uganda, Kenya, Tanzania, Burundi, and other neighboring countries.

These massacres marked an important turning point. They helped solidify a shift in the balance of power in the government from more inclusive politicians to those who wanted a Rwanda that clearly favored Hutus. Now firmly in power, these leaders believed the Tutsi presence outside of Rwanda threatened Hutu control. Moreover, the massacres provided a precedent for the state to use violence against the Tutsis as a political tool. While racial *tensions* had gradually increased under Belgian colonial rule, Tutsis had largely limited their *actions* to structural discrimination, while Hutus limited their responses to occasional intimidation and harassment. Now and for the future, state-sponsored violence would appear on the menu of political possibilities.

Kayibanda, however, would lose his position in the early 1970s. In 1972, the Tutsi-led government of neighboring Burundi engaged in **genocidal** violence against Hutus there. The racial dynamic in Burundi was similar to that in Rwanda, but in Burundi, Tutsis were the majority and Hutus the minority. Here, too, racial divisions were deep and here, too, they led to periodic violence. And in every case clashes in one country would reverberate in the other.

Genocide: "The attempt to destroy, in whole or in part, a racial, ethnical, religious or national group" (UN Convention on the Prevention and Punishment of the Crime of Genocide).

In 1973, in response to the persecution of Hutus in Burundi, Kayibanda again threatened Rwandan Tutsis. Unfortunately for Kayibanda, his plan backfired: The general he selected to lead the assaults against the Tutsis, Juvénal Habyarimana, instead led a coup that removed Kayibanda from power. Nevertheless, while only a few Tutsis were killed, it sent a message; another wave of elite Tutsis fled the country.

TIP

The resolution adopted by the UN Convention on the Prevention and Punishment of the Crime of Genocide, reprinted later in this game book, will come up repeatedly in the game. Read this document carefully.

Habyarimana would rule Rwanda as its president from 1973 until his death in 1994. In many ways, his regime represented a very real improvement for most Rwandans. He quickly stabilized the country politically. Socially and culturally, the government promoted (and enforced) mores of honesty, thrift, and Christian virtues (including the Catholic prohibition on birth control despite population growth of 3.7 percent per year, one of the highest in the world). Crime was virtually nonexistent. Even prostitution was tightly controlled and regulated.

The stability of Rwanda under Habyarimana made Rwanda an ideal candidate for foreign aid, which poured in throughout the 1970s and 1980s. France was the primary donor, but Belgium, Switzerland, and even the United States contributed as well. Consequently, the economy improved dramatically. In 1962, only two countries had **GNPs** lower than Rwanda; in 1987 there were eighteen. From this perspective, despite an increasing dependence on foreign aid (which we'll discuss later), the Habyarimana regime was incredibly successful.

Gross national product (GNP) is one measure of a country's prosperity. Roughly, this is the value of goods and services produced by a country in a year. By measuring how much a country makes in a year, the GNP gives a rough sense of how much wealth the people of a country have.

This success did not come without costs. The first was the monopolization of political power and government jobs by the Habyarimana regime. The *Mouvement Révolutionaire National pour le Développement* (the National Revolutionary Movement for Development, usually abbreviated MRND) was the only legal political party. All Rwandans were enrolled at birth in the party and remained members throughout their lives. To be sure, the party itself was far from homogenous. It was broken into unofficial factions, each largely determined by family or regional connections. Nevertheless, for ordinary Rwandans, the MRND shaped most aspects of their lives. Throughout the 1970s and 1980s, the state ran one-party elections, in which the candidate approved by the party routinely won by an overwhelming majority. The party/state monitored citizens' behavior to ensure they were acting "ethically" (for instance, women of loose morals risked arrest and reeducation, even when their actions weren't technically illegal). The government monitored where you lived—permission from the party was required to change residence—and where (and if) you went to school. As in colonial times, the government required its citizens to carry an identity card that listed one's race, although international human rights organizations occasionally tried to persuade the government to abandon this policy. The MRND required citizens to participate in weekly propaganda meetings and encouraged them to show respect for Habyarimana by wearing pins and ribbons or by hanging his picture in their houses.[10] Finally, the government continued the tradition of targeted violence against political enemies. While the numbers are small compared to those of other dictatorships, the Habyarimana government occasionally killed and more than occasionally imprisoned politicians or businessmen it found troublesome.

For those Tutsis still living in Rwanda, the Habyarimana government was a mixed bag. Habyarimana replaced the "national Hutuism" of the Kayibanda period with a system in which Tutsis were part of the national body, even if a second-class part, defined legally as a minority. Collective violence against Tutsis disappeared entirely and many Tutsis were free to run businesses and acquire wealth. They did so, however, at the cost of almost complete exclusion from the public sphere—namely from politics. There was a quota placed on Tutsis in universities and the civil service, although the percentage of Tutsis in universities was often above the expected 9 percent.[11] There were vanishingly small numbers of Tutsis in government; throughout the entire Habyarimana period, no Tutsis served as mayors or provincial leaders. Tutsi presence in the army was almost nonexistent. Between 1973 and 1990 there was only one Tutsi officer in the army, and Hutu soldiers were not allowed to marry Tutsis.

As we have seen, this stark division in Rwandan society had intellectual and legal precedents, rooted in a popular understanding of Tutsi and Hutu identities as fundamentally distinct. Not everyone in Rwanda saw this difference in the same way. Many Hutus understood Tutsis as Rwandan, but of a different kind. Under this logic, Hutus and Tutsis might be considered cousins, belonging to the same nation, but with different backgrounds and deserving different rights. Others still saw the difference through the lens of the Hamitic ideas first propagated during the colonial regime. In this view, Hutus considered Tutsis foreign invaders, aliens who didn't possess or deserve citizenship. At best, they were tolerated guests, at worst threats to a newfound Hutu security.

These intellectual debates didn't keep Hutus and Tutsis from marrying each other, living next to each other, or becoming friends. In particular, for ordinary people ethnicity played a much less visible role than it did for the elites, who had more power and resources and thus a bigger stake in the outcome. Nevertheless, these ideas about identity circulated among Rwandans throughout the Habyarimana period, available for anyone to draw on at times of confusion or crisis.

Just as Tutsi and Hutus carefully used rhetoric in their claims to power in society, Habyarimana talked about identity in the 1970s and early 1980s in ways both more moderate and more instrumental than is often imagined. Having taken power in a coup, his most important aims were to secure authority and solidify control. He quite consciously designed his public speeches and appearances to achieve this end. He downplayed regional and racial tensions in favor of emphasizing development and national unity. Whereas political imperatives had led Kayibanda to emphasize racial conflict in an attempt to solidify control, Habyarimana was pushed in a different direction. Rhetorical moderation—namely, downplaying racial tensions—would remain the norm as long as the Rwandan leadership was confident of its power.

Finally, these notions of identity shaped and were shaped by understandings of the meaning of democracy. Politically moderate Hutus emphasized their belief in the importance of elections and participation in government (even if the extent of that participation was limited). But they understood democracy in a particular way, one that equated democracy with the rule of the majority. Because the Tutsis were a minority, they had no claim to a role in making political decisions. Instead, elite Hutus should have total and absolute control. As a result, calls from Tutsi refugees abroad for the right to return were at best ignored. Simultaneously, these calls reinforced Hutu insecurities and lent urgency to warnings by Hutu extremists that the Tutsis represented an eternal enemy requiring eternal vigilance.

The Formation of the RPF

Tutsi refugees had adapted to life outside of Rwanda in many different ways. While the exact number of refugees is unclear, by 1990 there were perhaps 600,000 refugees scattered across Tanzania, Burundi, Zaire (now the Democratic Republic of the Congo) and Uganda. Of these, it was the refugees in Uganda that are most important for our story, as it was in Uganda that refugees managed to stage a significant military threat to Rwanda.

In Uganda, Rwandans had suffered with everyone else under the appalling dictatorship of Idi Amin in the 1970s and the successor regime of Milton Obote. In addition to the low-level abuses common under authoritarian regimes, government forces raped many native Ugandans and Tutsi refugees and stole thousands of cattle. While the government initiated and encouraged the violence, ordinary Ugandans gladly joined in.

TIP

Whether the Tutsis who fled in the 1960s and 1970s are refugees or foreigners will be important. If foreigners, they would have no right of return. Refugees, on the other hand, might plausibly claim the right to return and to regain the property seized from them after they left. Similarly—is the status of those who were old enough to have lived in Rwanda originally different from that of their children?

Many Tutsis responded by fleeing the country. Others, while remaining in Uganda, reacted to persecution by rediscovering the Rwandan identity of their parents. These Tutsis flooded into the National Resistance Army, a guerilla force opposing Obote, led by Yoweri Museveni. Museveni came from a tribe closely related to the Rwandan Tutsis, so it's unsurprising he welcomed refugees into his resistance force. Tutsi soldiers played a critical role in Museveni's defeating the Obote regime in 1986 and taking power in Uganda. In the aftermath of military victory, many of the Tutsi soldiers joined the new Ugandan army. Key individuals would eventually rise to high-ranking positions, most importantly Fred Rwigyema, who would become commander in chief and minister of defense, and Paul Kagame, appointed acting head of military security in 1990.

This small group of leaders would be instrumental in the crises of the next decade. Not content to remain in Uganda, they hoped and dreamed for a future in which they returned to Rwanda. The vehicle for this return would be the **Rwandan Patriotic Front** (**RPF**), a secret political and military party formed in 1987 that merged the Tutsi soldiers of the NRA with other refugee organizations. Rwigyema and his colleagues focused the RPF on two important goals. First, they wanted refugees to have the right to return to Rwanda and assurances that land would be available to them once they arrived there. Second, and equally important, they aimed to gain a significant share of political power within Rwanda. Toward these ends, they spent three years recruiting soldiers and acquiring access to weapons, munitions, and supplies of all kinds. These secured, they planned to wait for a moment of crisis, when they would then launch an attack against Rwanda.

Rwandan Patriotic Front (RPF): Organization of Tutsis living abroad with the goal of returning to Rwanda with full political rights there.

Rwanda in Crisis

That moment came in October 1990, when the RPF invaded Rwanda. A complicated mix of international politics, global economic trends, and political conflicts within Rwanda shaped the decision to attack at that specific moment. In Uganda, the RPF felt pressure to move quickly. In the months leading up to the invasion, international negotiations seemed to promise a path forward to resolving the refugee crisis. If refugees regained (or, children who had never stepped foot in their parents' homeland, gained) the right to live in Rwanda and felt safe doing so, it would deprive the RPF both of its reason for being and its core constituency. Invading Rwanda, then, would preempt these negotiations and secure the RPF's position.[12]

Just as important, though, was an economic and political crisis in Rwanda. The remarkable economic progress beginning in the 1950s collapsed in the 1980s and early 1990s. In part, this was due to explosive population growth that outstripped the agricultural capacity of the country. In the early 1990s, economists surveyed families living in a selected region of Rwanda. They found that, between 1988 and 1993, the percentage of households surveyed that owned less than a quarter hectare of land had risen from 36 percent to 45 percent (1 hectare is about 2.5 acres, so this is equivalent to owning less than two-thirds of an acre).[13] Put differently, the percentage of families in this area that could not grow enough food to feed themselves had risen 20 percent in only eight years. By the end of the 1980s, the World Bank counted Rwanda as one of the three worst agricultural performers in Africa.[14]

The agricultural challenge was exacerbated by a worldwide collapse in the price of coffee and tin that had begun in the mid-1980s. As both goods were important Rwandan exports, this badly damaged the country's economy. In 1985, Rwanda earned $144 million from coffee exports, by 1993 that number had plunged to $30 million.[15] Tin prices fell similarly. Employment levels and family incomes fell accordingly.

Finally, international donors demanded and secured cuts in the government's budget to prevent massive deficits. For example, the budget was slashed by 40 percent in 1989. The inevitable result was sizable and increasing budget deficits. In 1990, Rwanda ran a budget deficit equal to 12 percent of the Gross Domestic Product. In 1992 the figure was 18 percent and in 1994 an even larger 19 percent.[16]

At the national level, the fallout was startling. **GDP** per capita fell 5.7 percent in 1989 alone and continued its decline in the following years. Individual Rwandans, of course, suffered in individual ways, and their anger mounted until the crisis peaked in 1994. But it hit the political classes especially hard. Politicians and high-ranking government officials, already divided into regional and familial factions, had become accustomed to dividing a rather large pie. With the pie shrinking and world economic trends showing no signs of change, political division turned into political conflict.

Gross Domestic Product (GDP): A measure of how much a society makes in a year per person.

Finally, international donors began to call for a multiparty state and real democracy. Rwanda had been the darling of the international community in the 1970s and 1980s, as Habyarimana's ability to deliver consistent economic growth while avoiding cold war tensions allowed the West to ignore his authoritarian instincts. But in the new international atmosphere in 1989, donors began rethinking their priorities. Western powers no longer needed to support one-party states or oppressive regimes in the name of fighting the Soviet Union. Most notably, French President François Mitterrand announced in 1990 that French aid to African countries would flow "more enthusiastically" to countries that embraced democratic reforms. There were real questions about how seriously Mitterrand meant this statement, but leaders nevertheless recognized in it a very real change in the international environment.[17]

The combination of local and international demands for reform forced real change. After hesitating initially, Habyarimana announced in 1990 constitutional changes to pave the way for a multiparty system. In its wake, a variety of new parties formed, a new alphabet soup to which Rwandans soon became accustomed.

To a degree, honest men and women who favored representative government took the lead. More often, however, factions within the MRND simply transformed into parties without changing the underlying hunger for wealth and power. For that matter, the successor to the MRND, the newly dubbed MRNDD (National Movement for Development and Democracy) remained factionalized as well. Sometimes ideas drove people apart. Often, though, parties splintered along the regional divisions that had characterized Rwanda for decades. Whatever the reason, the fierce competition between and within parties that accompanied multiparty democracy quickly threatened to destabilize an already weak Habyarimana regime.

Promises of truly representative government also forced the RPF's hand. The fact that Habyarimana operated dictatorially was the RPF's best public relations weapon. Hope for a real democracy might win the enthusiastic support of Rwanda's citizens and deprive the RPF of any significant support within Rwanda and from the international community. RPF leaders understood that if they didn't attack Rwanda soon they might never again be in a position to do so successfully. It was now or never. Unsurprisingly, they decided to invade now.

The invasion itself, in October 1990, was quickly defeated. To some extent this was a matter of bad luck. A stray bullet killed the charismatic RPF commander Fred Rwigyema early on. Two other leading figures were killed in an ambush days after the invasion began. The new commander, Paul Kagame, would prove a capable leader, but the losses were significant blows. In addition, the RPF mistakenly chose to diverge from its original strategy, leaving it vulnerable to battlefield defeats. Finally, the RPF was outmanned and outgunned. Rwanda government forces, reinforced by supplies and troops sent from France, repulsed the RPF advance and drove it into the forests of Akagera National Park. Only a high-stakes attack that briefly captured the provincial city of Ruhengeri in January 1991 managed to salvage the prestige and position of the RPF. For the most part, the RPF was forced to operate using guerilla tactics for the following two years.

It says something about the political complexities of Rwanda that Habyarimana and the army knew an RPF invasion was coming and failed to prevent it. Museveni had expressed his concern to Habyarimana that an invasion was imminent. Habyarimana responded by attempting to infiltrate the RPF while simultaneously beginning negotiations to offer refugees a path home. However, the contest for power in Rwanda was a three-cornered game, with Habyarimana facing threats from both the RPF and the democratic opposition within the country. Indeed, the moderate opposition within Rwanda cooperated (albeit quietly and to a limited degree) with the RPF for some time after the invasion. Unwilling to make the concessions necessary to forestall an attack, Habyarimana apparently decided to gamble that an invasion would rally public opinion behind him instead of the opposition. Habyarimana's tactics extended to ordering the army to launch a fake attack on Kigali on October 4, 1990, to make an RPF victory seem imminent. He used this as an excuse to imprison hundreds of his political opponents.[18]

A brief word about the French intervention is necessary here. France had been a long-time ally of the Habyarimana regime. It negotiated military agreements as early as the 1970s to sell arms to Rwanda and brought French soldiers into Rwanda to train members of the FAR (the French acronym for the Rwandan national army). While these contracts did not imply or require active military support, the French government accepted Habyarimana's request for French troops in the days following the RPF's invasion, and several hundred French troops arrived shortly thereafter. They would not leave for some time and played an important role in halting the RPF in 1990.

The rest of the story can be told quite quickly. Within Rwanda, demands for multiparty democracy and for elections continued to mount. As they did, the infrastructure of public opinion and party democracy rapidly took shape, with newspapers, radio stations, and party publicity machines all multiplying quickly during 1991. Throughout, the regional divisions that had blossomed in the postcolonial period became increasingly prominent. Habyarimana continued to promise multiparty elections and democracy while doing everything he could to postpone actual progress and to distract the opposition leaders. These tensions continued throughout 1992 and into 1993.

These tensions also killed a problematic attempt to reach a compromise with the RPF. Prompted by the failing economy, Habyarimana agreed to sign a ceasefire in midsummer 1992, and negotiations began in the city of Arusha in neighboring Tanzania. Government negotiators seem to have sincerely hoped to reach an agreement. But neither the RPF nor the Rwandan government was willing at this stage to share power. Nor did **public opinion** in Rwanda favor negotiations at this point. Consequently, talks proceeded in fits and starts throughout the rest of 1992, with apparent breakthroughs in Tanzania vetoed in Kigali and by the RPF leadership.

Public opinion is the opinion of ordinary people as expressed to their politicians through letters, phone calls, and face-to-face encounters and as expressed in media outlets like newspapers and radio broadcasts.

TIP

Some of the players in the game will represent public opinion.

Simultaneously, issues of war and peace became political weapons in the broader debate over democratization, feeding the rise of extremism. By mid-1992 divisions within the new political parties were as significant as the differences between them. In each party, hardliners opposed moderates, and in each party, the moderates were on the retreat. Most parties were preparing for future battles by creating party militias, full of young men who found employment and personal satisfaction in carrying arms. Most famous of these militias was the Interahamwe (attached to Habyarimana's ruling party, the MRND). But almost every party had its own militia, tasked to defend its members and to support its goals.

With tensions high and the military situation stagnant, finding a meaningful agreement was virtually impossible. Thus when negotiators agreed on a power-sharing government in January 1993, the antipeace factions of all political parties erupted in violent protests. Over the next several days, approximately 300 people were killed. It seemed only a change in the military balance of power could break the diplomatic and political stalemate. Two weeks later, the RPF declared the cease-fire dead and renewed its attack.

This time the RPF was much more successful. Despite renewed French support (France shipped massive quantities of ammunition to the FAR and sent another 300 troops), the RPF occupied Ruhengeri and continued to advance. By February 20 it was within thirty kilometers of Kigali. It's impossible to know what would have happened if the RPF advance had continued. Some of the RPF high command wanted to proceed despite stiffening resistance and increasing French support of the Rwandan government forces. Even with the initial victories, Kagame, the RPF's leader, believed French support for the Rwandan government made further hostilities too risky. The RPF would return to the negotiating table. But it would, as the saying goes, keep its powder dry.

After six long months of further negotiations, both sides reached an agreement. The **Arusha Accords**, signed on August 4, 1993, outlined a process for concluding the war. In particular, it envisioned the formation of what the Accords called a Broad-Based Transitional Government (and a transitional national assembly), laid out procedures through which refugees could return and make claims to regain land lost when they fled Rwanda, and contained a power-sharing agreement through which RPF officers and soldiers would be incorporated into the FAR. It is important that it also called for the UN to create a peacekeeping force under Chapter 6 of the UN charter to supervise the implementation of the agreement.

Negotiators, especially on the Rwandan government's side, demanded a UN force because they knew full well the agreement they had signed would anger many hardline Hutus. Although both the RPF and the government made concessions, the accords seemed to favor the RPF in important ways. Moderates on both sides were afraid that hardline Hutus would work to undermine the agreement. The fears quickly proved correct. Politics in Rwanda, already punctuated by assassinations and protests, degenerated even further, with parties splintering, factions maneuvering for power, and Habyarimana searching desperately for support. All of this took place in a climate of increasingly open anti-Tutsi sentiment and persecution. Ominously, Hutu militias occasionally attacked Tutsi communities, killing, burning, and looting. The situation in Rwanda seemed to be getting worse, not better.

It was not so clear to the United Nations, however, which agreed to consider sponsoring a peacekeeping mission. Short on resources, it sent a skeletal investigation team to Africa. Ordinarily, a UN diplomat would lead such a team. However, the person Boutros Boutros-Ghali had in mind to lead the mission, Jacques-Roger Booh-Booh, was ill. In his place, the prospective military commander Roméo Dallaire, led the mission. In Rwanda the team was wined and dined by supporters of the agreement, who assured Dallaire repeatedly that this would be an easy mission. Arusha, they said, enjoyed the support of both sides. They just needed an impartial umpire to get them to the finish line. The UN would be it.

Dallaire later admitted that he and the UN were completely taken in. Dallaire, a Canadian general trained in peacekeeping, had little experience in diplomacy. Neither did the others on the team. They thus accepted much of what they were told at face value. Their report presented the undertaking as a straightforward peacekeeping mission, offering the UN an easy public relations opportunity at a time when the organization desperately needed one.[19] While there was some concern about the mission, particularly from the United States, the UNSC accepted Dallaire's recommendations and passed a resolution creating the **UN Assistance Mission for Rwanda (UNAMIR)** in October 1993.

UNAMIR's task got under way slowly. The Security Council authorized a force of about 2,500. Eventually, Belgium, Bangladesh, Ghana, and Tunisia stepped forward to offer troops to the mission. Of these, Belgian troops formed the effective core of UNAMIR, with the other contingents often individually capable, but undertrained and underequipped as a whole. Moreover, UNAMIR was chronically underfunded. Still, by late 1993 UNAMIR was a visible presence in Rwanda, even if it would take months to reach full strength. UNAMIR soldiers patrolled in and outside of Kigali, checked up on RPF and Rwandan army units, worked to gather intelligence about groups or individuals that might want to subvert the Arusha accords, and tried to mediate between Rwandan politicians and parties. All of this was important. But, given the size and resource challenges UNAMIR faced, none of it was transformational.

UN Assistance Mission for Rwanda (UNAMIR): A UN force created in October 1993 to monitor the Arusha accords in Rwanda.

Technically, the UN presence was more complicated than this, because the Security Council had sent a small number of observers to Rwanda earlier that summer. That level of detailed knowledge, however, isn't necessary to play the game.

In Rwanda, UNAMIR's exact job description was unclear. Its mission was to keep the peace. Reprising his role from 1993, Dallaire saw himself as a diplomat, working with Rwandan politicians to negotiate the transitional government and begin to implement Arusha. His men investigated armistice violations; observed rallies and riots; and gathered intelligence about hardline politicians, militias, and media.

As they did so, they stepped gingerly. Every UN mission was (and is) given careful instructions—technically called "Rules of Engagement"—by UN officials on what they can and can't do. These rules, for example, lay out when UN soldiers can use their weapons and against whom. In UNAMIR's case, the Rules of Engagement were somewhat ambiguous. They were not, however, perceived this way by UNAMIR commanders, who believed their soldiers could use their weapons only in self-defense.[20]

Despite UNAMIR's presence, the situation in Rwanda grew worse. Feuding between and within each of the several political parties, as well as within the RPF, repeatedly postponed the creation of the transitional government. Violence within Rwanda exploded, with repeated assassinations, noisy and often violent parades, rallies and speeches, and periodic attacks against the Tutsi minority. Habyarimana, as you'll remember, had encouraged unity throughout the 1970s and early 1980s. Now, he and other important politicians changed tactics. Instead of minimizing race, they claimed that all Tutsis supported the RPF and thus were traitors. Reminding people of the Hamitic thesis, they labeled Tutsis immigrants and argued they had no right to live in Rwanda. Recalling the earlier history of the country, they warned Hutus of what renewed Tutsi rule would be like. This rhetoric was often sincerely believed, but it was in all cases deployed strategically to defend a political position. And it represented a new and inflammatory addition to the political crisis.[21]

Meanwhile, events in nearby Burundi made matters even worse. Burundi, whose racial composition was a mirror image of that in Rwanda, had had its own political and racial problems since independence, problems that exploded into genocide in 1973 (when perhaps 200,000–300,000 Hutus were killed) and still simmered in the early 1990s.[22] For decades, events in one country reverberated in the other. In particular, Hutus and Tutsis in each country feared that massacres or repression in the other would spread to their own. The most important example of this feedback loop was the Tutsi-led coup in Burundi in October 1993. In that month, Tutsi officers in the Burundi army kidnapped and murdered the recently elected Hutu president of Burundi (an election hailed as a breakthrough in Burundian politics). In the aftermath, violence erupted throughout Burundi as Hutu peasants attacked their Tutsi neighbors and the Tutsi army cracked down on Hutus. Perhaps 50,000 were killed, while hundreds of thousands fled the country, many to Rwanda. Refugees worried that history would repeat itself in their new country. They often found a place in extremist party organizations or militia, which saw Rwanda in starkly racial terms, terms that seemed to validate their experience in Burundi. In the militia, they found something to do as well as a group of people who shared their current fears and hopes for the future. And they saw this fear reflected back at them by Rwandan politicians, who sought to use the racial violence for their own ends.[23]

It's important to recognize that these militias sometimes recruited by force or by peer pressure.

All in all, Rwanda in April 1994 was on the verge of political collapse. What would happen next was an open question. Everyone knew, however, the country was dancing on the edge of a volcano. The assassination of Habyarimana merely administered the final push.

THE UNITED NATIONS: A BRIEF HISTORY

You don't need to become an expert in the United Nations to play this game. However, it will help to learn a little bit about how and why the UN was created, what it does and doesn't do, and how that has changed over time. So get ready for a fast-paced trip through the history of the UN![24]

The League of Nations and the Birth of the UN

Taking a broad view, the UN emerged at a particularly difficult time in the history of the modern world. As the nineteenth century gave way to the twentieth, many in the West (the United States included) assumed the world had evolved past the frequent warfare that had plagued it for so long. Governments made decisions more rationally than before, they argued, and the growing interconnectedness of the world meant the costs of continued war would become intolerably high. World War I (1914–18), an agonizing conflict that resulted in 10 million dead and millions more wounded (even more if one counts the civil wars that lingered after the formal conclusion of the war), dispelled this illusion.

In the aftermath of World War I, some veterans and political leaders concluded that another war was inevitable. They turned their attention to preparing for that grim future. Others thought differently: that the world should not—could not—endure another such catastrophe. Accordingly, they argued, the very structure of the world order must change. Rather than individual powers acting in their own interest, a global organization would ensure some level of international cooperation and rule of law. Such a body would allow every country (or at least every Western country) to play a role in global decision making. When rogue nations took matters into their own hands, the new body would step in to bring those nations back into the fold.

That the advocates of shared governance would prevail was by no means inevitable. It is something of a fluke of history that its biggest supporter also happened to be the president of the United States. Woodrow Wilson was committed to a vision of an Americanized world, one in which many nations would have the right to participate in decisions made by a community of states designed to deter or oppose aggression. Many European leaders distrusted the idea. But, with Wilson holding all the cards—for America's foreign power arguably reached its zenith in the immediate postwar period—they had to give in. The result was the creation in 1919 of an international body called the League of Nations.[25]

With the League of Nations, the world embarked on an unprecedented experiment in cooperative decision-making. Ironically (and indeed disastrously for those who placed their hopes in the new organization), the United States refused to join. Many Americans feared a global council would infringe on American sovereignty (this important concept is discussed more fully later in this section). Others believed American interests would be best served by sidestepping interactions with the rest of the world. In the face of such opposition, Wilson failed to convince the U.S. Senate to join the League of Nations. It would become one of the greatest frustrations of his life.

Whether American membership would have offered the League a better chance for success in the events that followed is needless speculation. For the world posed many more challenges than the League was equipped to handle. In particular, several world-historical events in this period would have challenged even the most capable of leaders—for example, the collapse of the Russian and Austro-Hungarian empires in the aftermath of World War I, Germany's unwillingness to accept its defeat; the financial costs of the war; the Great Depression of the 1930s; and above all, the inability of people to come to grips with an ever-increasing pace of social, technological, and political change. It is no disrespect to good people doing their best to say the leaders of the League of Nations were ordinary rather than extraordinary. It's not really a surprise that such an experiment failed under the stresses of a global crisis. Nor is it a surprise that the next war would be even more destructive than the last.

This war would come to be known as World War II (1939–45). It pitted Germany, Italy, and, eventually, Japan against France, the United Kingdom, and eventually, the Soviet Union and the United States. In some ways this war was just a bigger, more destructive version of World War I. Where 10 million soldiers died in the first war, over 20 million died in the second. But in other ways, it was far worse. The combatants of World War I had sometimes treated civilians badly. Germany, the Soviet Union, Japan, and some others did so as a matter of policy. Although estimates vary, it is not unreasonable to suggest that 50 million civilians perished during the war. Race played a role around the edges of the first war but would play an increasingly larger role in the second: Attempts to create a utopian future meant that Germany and (sometimes) its allies tried to eliminate Jews and some other groups from the earth. World War I introduced tanks, airplanes, submarines, and poisonous gas to the battlefield; World War II ended with the dropping of two atomic bombs, each of which unleashed the destructive power of more than 15,000 tons of TNT. If witnesses to the first war thought it devastating, observers of the second wondered if humankind itself could survive a third.

The name **United Nations** came from the label the Allies against Germany had adopted during the war.

Even though the League of Nations had collapsed in the late 1930s, having failed to prevent the onset of war, many continued to think in terms of collective security. In the midst of World War II, leaders of the countries fighting against Germany considered how to craft a new global organization. Discussions accelerated as victory over Germany became first likely and then certain. Strikingly, while fighting against Germany and Japan continued, the Allies drafted a vision for the United Nations Organization in late 1944. Discussions continued over the following months, leading to the signing of the UN Charter, its founding document, in June 1945 and the official creation of the United Nations in October of that same year.

Founding the UN: Visions and Institutions

The founders of the UN had very different visions. Some saw it as a resurrection of the nineteenth-century Concert of Europe, a system of conflict resolution that had evolved among European powers to ensure that sovereign countries tried first to solve global challenges through careful negotiation and bargaining. Other UN founders, convinced a rational world must be a peaceful one, viewed the new organization as a distinctly twentieth-century institution, one that would finally bring the rationality of science to bear on global governance. Still others envisioned the UN as a way to divide the responsibility for global security among the great powers.

It didn't help that the leaders of the wartime alliance had distinct, often contradictory, goals. The so-called Big Three were Winston Churchill, the British prime minister; Joseph Stalin, the leader of the Soviet Union; and Franklin Roosevelt, the president of the United States. These leaders played the most important role in designing the UN, and while doing so each tried to advance the interests of their own country. To the extent that a United Nations would accomplish the goals its founding countries deemed important, the Big Three were happy to craft such an organization. But the devil is in the details, and each had different visions for how the UN should be structured, what kinds of power it should have, and who should lead it. Moreover, Churchill and Roosevelt each had to consider voters in their home countries potentially hostile to such an organization.

The UN that emerged from months of negotiations reflected these varying goals and commitments. The preamble laid out a beautiful vision of a world where war was no more, justice reigned, and international collaboration ensured prosperity and stability. It spoke of "international cooperation," "friendly relations between nations," and especially about "maintaining international peace and security." Quickly, however, the Charter made it clear this language was meant to limit the UN rather than empower it. For instance, Article 2 made clear the UN was committed to preserving the sovereignty of member states and that members had no right to interfere in the domestic affairs of another country. In essence, the founders intended the UN to prevent another world war, not to solve all the problems of the world.

TIP

Understanding the rights and purpose of the UN is critical to the game. Pay close attention to this section and the UN Charter that you will read online (see p. 78).

The founders proceeded to build institutions that implemented their vision. The General Assembly provided a place for all member nations to discuss matters of common interest. Additional economic agreements and structures (to which most of the powers agreed at an earlier summit at Bretton Woods, New Hampshire) laid out a strategy to manage the global economy and prevent a return to the Great Depression. In each case, there was at least the appearance of respect for the desires and rights of every independent country. In the crucial matter of making and carrying out security policy, however, the situation was very different. Each of the Big Three feared an activist UN would infringe on their own security interests. Moreover, it was clear that only a few states had the power and the will to intervene in international disputes. To use Roosevelt's phrase, these powers would have to be the "policemen" of the new international order. Given this reality, getting the Big Three to agree to any real kind of security structure would require special guarantees.

The result was the UN Security Council (the UNSC). This body was composed of six rotating member nations, each serving two-year terms. (This number would later increase; in 1994, when this game is set, there were 10 members, and today there are 15.) Five permanent powers (customarily referred to as the P5) joined the rotating members on the UNSC: France, China, the United Kingdom, the United States, and the Soviet Union (Russia succeeded the Soviet Union in the early 1990s). Regardless of how these countries fared after the war or whether they used their position responsibly, these countries would stay on the UNSC forever.

The voting procedure was also skewed to privilege the P5. Any member of the council could place an item on the agenda. But, when it came time to vote, member states were definitely not equal. To pass the council, at least 60 percent of the member states had to vote in support of the motion. However, if *any* of the permanent members voted against the motion, the motion failed. Colloquially known as a veto, this gave an enormous amount of power to the P5 in determining policy. The P5 might have chosen to use this power sparingly, but they did not. The language of the Charter leaves some ambiguity about what kinds of votes are subject to the veto. But the practice quickly emerged of assuming the veto was universally applicable. When the ambassador of a smaller country asked the Soviet ambassador how to decide which issues were subject to the veto, his terse response was telling. After listening to the question, the Soviet simply replied, "We shall tell you."[26]

If conflict threatened or erupted between member states, the Charter gave the Security Council a broad range of options. It might encourage countries to engage in peace talks or arbitration. It might condemn actions taken by one or more combatants. It might commit its members to economic sanctions. Or it might decide to use force to bring an end to armed conflict. In that case, it had two broad options. The first, laid out in Chapter 6, addresses situations in which conflict has ended and combatants are committed to a peace process. Here, the UN's role is to facilitate the process—observing armistices, collecting arms, monitoring elections, arbitrating disputes, and so on. In such a case, the UN might commit forces to the region, but they are not expected to need or use their weapons. Peace is in sight and the UN's role is to make sure nothing stands in the way. Over time, people began referring to this as a Chapter 6 mandate or, more informally, peacekeeping.

But there would be times when one or both of the warring states didn't want the war to end (at least not yet). In this case, the founders envisioned a UN able to *make* peace, not just administer it. The process for this was laid out in Chapter 7 and hence is usually called a Chapter 7 mandate (over time, people started to talk about this as peacemaking). Simply declaring a Chapter 7 action wouldn't necessarily require an armed invasion. It might be (or at least begin as) a nonviolent coercion, implementing an embargo or other kinds of trade sanctions or targeting the freedom of movement of national leaders. Or it might use force at a distance, for instance by mounting a blockade. But it at least allowed and often required the UN to deploy troops into the conflict zone.

One might assume from this the UN needed its own armed force. Indeed, there was much discussion about the creation of an international army or air force. Ultimately, however, the founders rejected this. Instead, they included in the charter an expectation that member states would (*not* should) stand prepared to provide troops to implement Security Council decisions. To increase the UN's military capacity, the United States pledged to create a series of army, navy, and air force bases throughout the world that would be placed at the disposal of the UN. Other nations were invited to supplement these with their own bases and logistical structures.

The logical next question became who would command, organize, and administer these forces. Originally, the Security Council was to possess its own **general staff**, made up of the chiefs of staff of the P5 powers, which would advise and assist the Security Council in all matters related to the use of armed forces. They might (but only *might*) invite the military leaders of other countries to offer support or advice.

General staff: A permanent organization within a branch of the military (army, navy, and so on) that has authority over planning and strategy.

To complete our picture of the UN at its founding, we need to look at two more issues. First, the UN needed some kind of administrator. Given the title of secretary-general, this position was initially regarded as limited and administrative. He (so far, all of the secretary-generals have been men) ran the Secretariat—the bureaucracy that carried out the work of the General Assembly, the Security Council, and the other bodies of the UN. In addition, he served as a kind of research assistant for the UN, especially the Security Council. It is important that he had the authority to introduce issues onto the agenda of the Security Council, offering another path by which crises might be brought to the attention of that body; however, he was not expected to be a leader or executive, just an administrator.

Second, shortly after the war, the UN passed an agreement, called, in the arcane language of the UN, a convention that carved out a narrow but important exception to the principle of state sovereignty. The Convention on the Prevention and Punishment of the Crime of Genocide passed quite unexpectedly, mostly due to the passion, energy, and political skill of Polish refugee and lawyer Raphael Lemkin.[27] You will read the convention in the course of preparing for this game and your GM will almost certainly discuss it with you. For now, it's worth pointing out that its vision limiting the rights of states contrasts significantly with the original UN Charter. Because of this, the degree to which UN members really supported the Genocide Convention is open to question. Passed in 1948, individual countries took years or decades to ratify it. The United States, for instance, ratified the convention only in 1986 (and passed the necessary legislation to implement the treaty still later).

For all of the debate surrounding the founding of the UN and its institutions, some things were clear. There was broad agreement the League of Nations had failed because it could not compel countries to follow the covenant. The United Nations had to be able to enforce its judgments, or it would face the same fate. But how would an institution born out of a global war fare after the war was over?

The UN during the Cold War

No one expected the P5 would always get along. But few anticipated how quickly the wartime alliance would collapse. Nor did they foresee the emergence of the

Cold War: The competition between the Soviet Union (with its allies) and the United States (with its supporters) lasting roughly from the late 1940s until the late 1980s.

Cold War, which left the United States and the Soviet Union reflexively opposing each other at every step. This antagonism effectively destroyed the founders' hopes for the UN.

Most important, the vision of the UN acting collectively to prevent or contain international conflict never got off the ground. For the Security Council to work at all, countries had to use the veto sparingly, a last resort employed only when a nation's vital interests were at risk. But during the Cold War the United States and the Soviet Union each saw the other as an existential threat. In this environment, policy makers quickly began to view the world in black and white. If a country was on your side, its prosperity, borders, and stability became essential to your own success or failure. If it was not, it was automatically on the other side and thus a threat to your own existence. Starting from that assumption, it became impossible for the Security Council to evaluate international conflicts rationally and impartially. And so the council's workings quickly ground to a halt.

That doesn't mean the council stopped altogether. Instead, meetings became places to score points. When the council seemed on the brink of actually doing something, the United States or the Soviet Union used its veto power to protect their respective allies. They did this repeatedly, rendering the council powerless when conflict broke out. The exception to that, the Korean War (1950–53), proves the rule. The UN intervened against North Korea only because the Soviet Union was boycotting the Security Council at the time and did not cast a vote. It was a lesson neither side ever forgot.

The stalemate led to a significant change in the role of the secretary-general. Originally a supporting player, the secretary-general now took on an entirely new role. In crises of global significance, the UN took a back seat to diplomacy conducted by the United States, the Soviet Union, and other influential countries. But that left a wide variety of crises too small or too controversial to interest the great powers. Activist secretaries-general—such as the widely praised Dag Hammarskjöld, a Swede—stepped in and carved out a much more important role for their office than originally intended. By the end of the cold war, the secretary-general had become the public face of the UN, laying out and guarding the organization's vision. He was its lead negotiator in cases of international conflict. And it was his role (not always an easy one or always accomplished effectively) to mediate disagreements between the great powers.

Another consequence was the erosion of American support for the UN. Whether the American public would accept an active role in the UN had always been an open question. This influenced the way Roosevelt approached negotiations over the shape of the perspective United Nations and the way he presented the organization to the electorate. While public opinion remained divided, his intensive campaign initially persuaded a majority of Americans to support both the concept and reality of American participation. But this support gradually eroded. In particular, the widespread American perception that the UN was anti-Israel played an important role in souring public opinion, feeding into a broad and increasing perception that the UN was slanted against American interests. Over time, more countries joined the UN. These were usually poor, formerly colonized nations, and often to the left of the United States in political orientation. This meant the United States was consistently outvoted in the General Assembly. Many Americans saw this as evidence that the UN was the enemy.

As a result, when the politics of the Security Council tilted against American interests in the late 1960s, the United States was forced to use the veto again and again. Previously, the Soviet ambassador had cast veto after veto in both security and procedural matters. But then the situation reversed completely. Between 1985 and 1990, the United States cast an astounding twenty-seven vetoes. To be sure, for some Americans dubious about the UN, the existence and use of the veto in fact validated American membership. It meant, in the words of American Senator Vandenberg, "the system worked."[28] But for most, it was another sign the UN primarily served the interests of others, not the United States.

Americans also increasingly complained about the amount of money their nation was expected to pay. While every member nation had a vote in the General Assembly, the rich countries contributed by far the most to the UN budget. The United States, as the richest country in the world, was asked to pay far more than others. While the actual amount America paid was negligible compared to its overall budget (and, in fact, it usually declined to pay the entire amount expected of it), it became a constant irritant in U.S.–UN relations and just another reason Americans doubted the UN's competence and raison d'être.

Moreover, Americans often believed the money they did contribute was being wasted. As the decades continued, the size and cost of elements of the UN bureaucracy skyrocketed. In large part, this occurred precisely because the UN was a membership organization. Each member wanted a seat at every table and jobs for its own citizens. As a result, the complexity and inefficiency of the UN bureaucracy became legendary. While simple requests took weeks or months to process, office after office seemed full of officials who did nothing. It's certainly possible to argue that Americans (and other critics) exaggerated the UN's inefficiency, but it's hard to argue that the problem itself was entirely imaginary.

Finally, the Cold War meant the collapse of plans to create a military infrastructure for the UN. No one doubted the need to build its military capacity, but the atmosphere in the UN made actually creating it a nonstarter. Absent its own military, the UNSC first assumed the P5 would contribute the vast majority of forces to any UN intervention. But because during the Cold War the United States and the Soviet Union were at loggerheads, this would almost never happen (Korea, again, is a notable exception). As a result, it was mostly smaller countries that ended up supplying troops to UN missions. Sometimes these came from the few countries that considered peacekeeping fundamental to the mission of their armed forces (Canada, for instance). Sometimes countries with a historical interest and involvement in a particular region offered troops. Often, however, countries desperate for cash essentially rented their troops to the UN. Accordingly, forces differed wildly in levels of training, equipment, and motivation. It surprised no one when these forces found it difficult to achieve their missions.

Thus, by the 1980s, even sympathetic observers had to acknowledge that the UN had not fulfilled the grand hopes of its founders. Whether that was inherent in the UN's design or simply a product of the Cold War remained to be seen.

The UN after the Cold War

The end of the Cold War, usually dated as 1989 but in fact a process that began in the late 1980s and continued into the early 1990s, surprised everyone. For those who didn't live through the heights of the Cold War, it's hard to imagine the jubilation, excitement, and sheer relief felt in the late 1980s. This was true in the United States and among its allies, no longer confronted daily with the remote but never-absent possibility of nuclear war. It was also true in the so-called Third World, which could now imagine an autonomy possible only when the great powers didn't really care about them anymore. It was particularly true in eastern Europe, where people in country after country reclaimed power for themselves after wresting it from the now-former Soviet Union.

The year 1989 became a symbol as much as a reality: It meant a new beginning. It meant the end of history, to paraphrase Francis Fukuyama's famous declaration.[29]

This claim was much ridiculed and just as much misunderstood. Fukuyama didn't mean history was literally over. Rather, he meant that history, understood as the story of how humans governed themselves, led inevitably to a world that believed democracy the only appropriate way for humans to govern themselves. People (if not their rulers) across the world accepted this claim, if not the philosophy behind it, that international governance should start with the sovereign state, under the oversight of the United Nations.

They meant three things by this. First, and most simply, most thought the world should be run by an international community, not held hostage by two superpowers (or, now, one). The greatest symbol of this was President George H. W. Bush, who publicly encouraged the emergence of a community of states that would share in governing/supervising the world. But Bush's was merely one voice in a broader consensus that it was finally the UN's moment.

Second, many concluded that democracies were simply better for citizens than authoritarian governments. Democracies didn't fight other democracies, the saying went. Democracies were less likely to go to war in general and in particular were less likely to oppress their own people than were other kinds of governments. As Michael Barnett wrote, "international order is premised on domestic order, domestic order is contingent on the state being viewed as legitimate by its society, states are most legitimate when they operate with the consent of their societies and honor the rule of law, and the principles of consent and the enshrinement of the rule of law are tantamount to democracy."[30] Thus building democratic institutions and cultures became a means toward the broader end of the United Nations.

Finally, for many the end of the Cold War was a triumph for the idea of human rights—the claim that we have rights simply because we are human (rather than because we are citizens of a state.[31] This idea has a long history; it suffices here to point out this was the first time in world history that many people had accepted such a claim in a political (rather than religious) context. With human rights as a governing logic that transcended citizenship or faith, the UN, as a global association of nations, became in some people's eyes their natural guarantor.

These assumptions implied, indeed required, a more active and powerful UN to complete the post-1989 transition to the new world. This would create several growing pains; we'll consider two of them.

Security Costs One result of the UN's expanded role was an almost immediate jump in the number of UN peacekeeping missions. In the forty years before 1989, the UN had engaged in thirteen peacekeeping operations. Even this number is misleading, as there were only three new missions in the 1970s and none at all between 1980 and 1987. But in the period from 1988 to 1993, the UN added about twenty new peacekeeping missions. Between 1987 and 1994, the number of deployed peacekeepers leapt from 10,000 to 70,000, and the budget required to support them increased from $230 million to $3.4 billion.[32] The cost was widely accepted as the price of a newly relevant, newly active UN.

A new secretary-general both embodied and encouraged this attitude. Boutros Boutros-Ghali, a formerly obscure Egyptian, now possessed a bully pulpit. He used it to cast a vision of a future[33] in which the UN separated combatants, facilitated negotiations, observed elections, and promoted democracy. (In informal terms, it was as if the UN had become some combination of policeman and marriage counselor for the world.) It would accomplish this successfully because it had learned the lessons of decades of experience in peacekeeping. In doing so, it would bring the world closer to peace and prosperity for all.

Unnoticed, however, were the seeds of institutional and philosophical disaster. For one, the UN lacked the institutional capacity to carry out such a broad mandate. The UN was famous for its bureaucratic culture, one that seemed to require an endless series of signatures from a never-ending series of officials. But, in fact, the UN's peacekeeping arm was dramatically understaffed. As you'll remember, the founders envisioned a permanent military staff for the UN, a dream never realized. In its place, secretaries-general had crafted a number of ad-hoc bodies, which had never truly sufficed.

Immediately after his appointment, Boutros-Ghali began to put his own stamp on this aspect of the UN. In particular, he created in 1992 two distinct bodies to carry out Security Council mandates. The Department of Political Affairs and the Department of Peacekeeping Operations (DPKO) were supposed to divide along functional lines—with the former taking responsibility for vision and grand strategy while the latter executed that vision. In principle, this made sense, but never really worked in practice. For one, the two bodies often clashed over responsibility and authority: The line between strategy and execution sounded neat but was in reality quite blurry. Moreover, Boutros-Ghali's intentions were more political than administrative. He believed the P5 had long exerted too much control over UN operations. By creating two distinct offices for peacekeeping, he hoped to isolate P5 influence in the office he believed less important, the DPKO. The Department of Political Affairs, then, would offer him advice and control untainted by P5 (especially American) goals and priorities. The result, however, was confusion. The two agencies refused to share information, competed for influence, and in general complicated operations rather than simplifying them.[34]

Exacerbating the structural problems, the increase in the number and size of UN operations was nowhere near matched by an increase in capacity. The DPKO in 1994 had about fifty officers, far below the number needed to successfully supervise operations under its control. Similarly, the end of the Cold War did nothing to persuade the P5 to provide forces dedicated full-time to the UN. As a result, each individual mission was staffed with troops speaking a variety of languages, coming from a variety of institutional cultures, and bringing with them a variety of equipment and levels of training. Efficiency and effectiveness were hardly the most likely outcomes.

Moreover, the momentary resurgence of American support for the United Nations quickly faded. Bush's desire to craft a new kind of international order was hardly universal. But the demands of the UN's newly active role in world affairs, and its seeming inability to do anything effectively, rapidly eroded that limited support. As suggested earlier, the United States had for many years chafed at its required contribution to the general budget of the UN. But the budget for peacekeeping operations was separate from the general budget. By the early 1990s, the peacekeeping budget was two to three times the size of the "ordinary" budget. And the United States paid 28 percent of these expenses. Many in other countries believed the size of the American economy and America's ability to wield the veto justified this figure. But by the early 1990s American politicians, especially Republicans, called repeatedly for America's contribution to be renegotiated. If it was not, they threatened, they would simply refuse to pay the bill. In a period where the UN teetered on bankruptcy several times, this was a potent threat.

Role in Internal Conflicts The other challenge faced by the UN in its new global role was the emergence of an entirely new mission and context for peacekeeping and peacemaking. The UN was built on the assumption that the world was composed of sovereign states. Its role, then, was to limit conflicts between states. Civil wars represented the one real exception to this assumption. Even this could be reasoned away, for civil wars were either internal conflicts over power, and thus not within the purview of the UN, or were conflicts between two separate peoples and thus in fact a kind of international conflict.

No one anticipated a world in which states simply collapsed. Yet, this was the world that seemed to be emerging in the late twentieth century. Partly a product and legacy of cold war conflicts, partly a result of the way decolonization occurred, and partly stemming from institutional failure, governance in a number of countries simply collapsed. What happened in the wake of this collapse varied, but it was never good. Sometimes warlords established regional governments that thumbed their noses at their own and other governments. In other cases, peoples seceded and tried desperately to rule themselves. In the worst places, gangs, warlords, and drug lords waged endless, and endlessly violent, struggles for power and resources, leaving the general population vulnerable to exploitation, starvation, rape, and murder.

As we have seen, the UN was not designed or intended to solve these kinds of problems. But the new logic of the post–Cold War international order demanded action. So the vast majority of UN peacekeeping operations following 1989 were state-building or humanitarian operations, not operations designed to keep two warring states apart.

These operations were fraught with hazards. At best, UN forces dealt with a weak government obsessed with shoring up its authority. At worst, UN peacekeepers were forced to negotiate simultaneously with a variety of forces, many of which viewed the UN as an unwanted intruder into local politics. In either case, UN commanders had to face these challenges undersupplied and understaffed. It was a recipe for failure, if not disaster.

Somalia pushed the UN to the breaking point. A complicated civil war in Somalia had led to the collapse of centralized authority and the emergence of local militias, perhaps better labeled "gangs," competing for power and resources. By mid-1991, this left most Somali cities in ruins and hundreds of thousands of refugees displaced. As the economy disintegrated, the specter of mass starvation emerged. All of this played out on the television screen, as networks freed from covering cold war competition now paid more attention to crises in the developing world.[35]

In the new, media-saturated age, the UN and its governments could not ignore the suffering. But neither could it come up with a solution that would be simultaneously cheap, safe, and effective. As initial attempts failed, the UN gradually increased its commitment. By mid-1992, there were 500 peacekeepers in Somalia trying desperately to distribute food and medicine. But that aid was quickly confiscated by the local militias. Soon, television showed images of well-fed young men driving pickups with machine-guns mounted in back parked next to young girls and boys suffering visibly from hunger and disease. By the end of 1992, about half a million people had died.

Backed into a corner, the UN came out swinging. An initial peacekeeping force, arriving in the country in spring of 1992, proved too small to be effective. So the UN doubled down, deciding in December 1992 to dispatch an American task force to Somalia to make real humanitarian relief possible. Once ashore, this force found itself at the center of a debate over Somalia's future. It was not enough, many policy makers argued, to save people today. The UN must reconstruct Somalia as a modern country with a unified government that could lead its people into the twenty-first century. To do this, the UN must intervene in the civil war, forcing the combatants to the negotiating table and punishing those who refused. American military and political leaders were unenthused by this project. But Boutros-Ghali and other UN leaders were determined to make a difference. And so *nation building* (to use the newly popular term) began in earnest.

The result was an escalating spiral of conflict between UN forces and the local warlords. In particular, General Aidid, a Somali warlord who claimed to be the next leader of Somalia, rejected the UN's presence. In July 1993, Aidid decided to raise the stakes. His forces ambushed and killed twenty-four Pakistani peacekeepers. Enraged, the UN decided Aidid had to go and began efforts to hunt him and his allies down. The Americans took the lead in implementing this mandate.

Battle of Mogadishu: The failed attempt to capture members of a militia, which led to the deaths of eighteen American peacekeepers. Portrayed in the movie *Black Hawk Down.*

This effort went tragically awry in an enormously important raid on October 3, now known as the **Battle of Mogadishu.** American rangers landed by helicopter at a hotel housing several Somali leaders allied with Aidid. The raid initially went well. But soon, hundreds of angry Somalis gathered around the hotel. As the rangers tried to return to the base with their captives, the Somalis began to shoot at the Americans. By the time the action was over, 18 American soldiers were dead and 78 wounded while between 500 and 1,000 Somalis had been killed or wounded. While the casualties were clearly tragic, most important in terms of public opinion was undoubtedly the video of a dead American soldier being dragged through the streets of Mogadishu while thousands of Somalis cheered.

The events in Mogadishu reverberated throughout the world. Public opinion, already dubious of UN peacekeeping missions, turned actively hostile. American politicians, especially Republicans, attacked President Clinton for having sacrificed American soldiers on the altar of an international organization (see the speech by Jesse Helms on p. 139 in this game book). Clinton, in turn, tried to shift the blame to the UN and its leadership. Prominent newspapers and television programs called for defunding the UN and for refusing to provide troops for UN missions, calls echoed by congressmen and senators. Global response was more mixed. But even in places that responded more moderately than the United States did, one thing seemed clear. The short era of the UN seemed to be over.

So, after our journey through the history of the UN, what are the takeaways for you as you think about the game? There are several. First, the capacity and authority of the UN rarely matched the soaring rhetoric of the UN Charter. Second, the UN's "moment," when it enjoyed widespread acclaim and could move countries to action, was, if not over, at least in danger of being over by the end of 1993. The natural response was to hesitate before taking up any mission carrying any significant risk. Third, it was becoming apparent that the challenges of nation building and peacekeeping were many and varied. At the same time, the capacity of the UN to engage in these operations, while improving, remained remarkably limited. Talks of reforming the DPKO, of instituting more standardized processes and Rules of Engagement, and of more expanding the UN's capacity to mobilize forces were at a very preliminary stage and much contested.

BOSNIA AND THE ROLE OF UN PEACEKEEPING

Why, in a game about Rwanda, do you need to read anything about Bosnia? The answer is simple: Rwanda's collapse didn't occur in a vacuum. Much to the contrary, Rwanda exploded at the busiest period in the UN's short history. In real life, the time in which the game is set saw the UNSC beset with multiple demands, demands that often seemed more urgent than those from Rwanda. There's no way to replicate this in the game, although you can assume some players will want to talk about issues other than Rwanda. Bosnia was merely the most important of the many crises of 1994 and was uppermost in the mind of many policy makers. Accordingly, you'll need a bit of background knowledge to respond appropriately. In particular, players looking to make an argument that prioritizes national security as a criterion for intervention should read this section carefully and then do more research.

Legacy of Yugoslavia

Yugoslavia emerged in 1918 in the aftermath of World War I out of the remnants of the Habsburg monarchy and several small independent countries in the Balkans. Its roots lay in prewar agitation by those who believed that the Serbs, Croats, and Slovenes were nations (or ethnic groups) and therefore deserved to control their own fate. Its original name, the Kingdom of the Serbs, Croats, and Slovenes, suggested some of the dynamics that would plague the country for the next eighty years. The name implied a confederation of three different peoples (or, alternately, ethnic groups). For many of its citizens, that's exactly what it was. But others believed the Serbs, Croats, and Slovenes were actually brothers, that each was a member of a broader family of peoples called the South Slavs. The name change to Yugoslavia, which happened in 1929, was both a recognition of the success of the proponents of this vision and an effort to teach unbelievers their true identity. Either way, the kingdom existed because its leaders thought nations deserved states.

The tensions between the two visions continued throughout Yugoslavia's existence. At times, for instance, from 1929 to 1941, hostilities remained hidden. At times, they broke into the open, most obviously from 1941 to 1945, during the German occupation of the region in World War II. This period saw a vicious three-way contest between Germans and their allies, Yugoslav monarchists, and Communists. The violence was most obvious and most intense in the Independent State of Croatia, a puppet state created by Germany and run by a local fascist party, the Ustaše. The Ustaše government tried hard to cleanse its new country of all Serbs and many Jews. Concentration camps, rapes, shootings, and torture all formed part of the Ustaše toolkit. Tens, possibly hundreds, of thousands of people perished during the violence. The casualty count outside of Croatia was lower, but the fighting just as bitter. Each side fought the other two, each side took no prisoners, and each side played to win.

In the aftermath of the war, its victors, the Yugoslav communists under Josip Tito, managed to repress wartime ethnic violence and to pretend the atrocities had never happened. Tito was a child of a mixed marriage (his father was Croat and his mother Slovene) who joined the Communist Party of Yugoslavia shortly after World War I ended. Whether because of his ancestry or because of communism's rejection of ethnic identities, Tito identified himself as a Yugoslav and a communist throughout his life. Tito led Yugoslavia from 1945 until his death in 1980. He strove throughout that period to instill in people an allegiance to Yugoslavia rather than to Croatia or Serbia or Slovenia. He never quite succeeded in eliminating ethnic identities and tensions completely. But for much of Tito's period in power, these tensions remained underground, never completely gone but never quite open.

Tito's death in 1980 opened up a space for these memories to reemerge. Tito's role as Yugoslavia's liberator had made him uniquely able to command support for his ideas. His death left a political vacuum that nationalist politicians rushed to fill. Serbs, Croats, and Slovenes within Yugoslavia each talked openly about protecting their own ethnic group against the political demands and powers of the others. Some, like the Croats and Slovenes, wanted independence. Others, such as the Serbs under their nationalist leader Slobodan Milošević, wanted to cement Serbian leadership and power within a reorganized Yugoslavia. All rejected the conception of Yugoslavia as a nation where all South Slavs could live together as brothers and sisters.

The final brake on demands for secession was the Soviet control over Eastern Europe. When that collapsed in 1989, Yugoslavia slowly fell apart. Slovenia, small and ethnically coherent, was the first to go in June 1991. Yugoslav leaders put up a token resistance to the Slovenian decision but quickly allowed it to go its own way. Croatian demands for independence were considerably more problematic. Croatia was larger and richer. More important, Croatians and Serbs lived mixed in the borderlands between the two provinces. Unless these populations were somehow forced to separate, independence would inevitably leave Croatia and/or Serbia with a significant minority population. Unwilling to see his dreams of a greater Serbia die and equally unwilling to allow Serbs to live under a Croatian government, Milošević and the Yugoslav army intervened, and a fierce war erupted between the two. The armies fought not just over territory, but over people, as each attempted to change the human geography of the region. They did so through massacres, rapes, and deportations—what became known as ethnic cleansing. Quickly, Europeans and Americans began to see stories of this violence on their television screens and in newspapers. While this war would continue for another four years, it quickly became obvious that Milošević's dreams of a Serbian-dominated Yugoslavia were impossible. Instead, he (and other Serb leaders) decided the next best thing was a large independent Serbia to include Serb-populated areas of the former Yugoslavia. The most obvious target was Bosnia.

Bosnia was a microcosm of all of Yugoslavia's potential and all of its problems. Bosnia had long been multiethnic and multireligious, with Orthodox Serbs, Catholic Croatians, and Muslim Bosnians intermingled. Although an awareness of difference never disappeared, they had lived relatively peacefully for decades. In 1991 and 1992, however, nationalist leaders within Bosnia (particularly the

Bosnian Serb Radovan Karadžić) cooperated with Milošević and Croatian president Franjo Tuđman to lead Bosnia into a civil war.[36] Serbia and Croatia seized on the fighting as an excuse to intervene. Again, this was fought with no concern for the laws of war. Serb soldiers looted and raped both for personal satisfaction and as tactics in a broader campaign of ethnic cleansing. If Serbia and Croatia could drive the Bosnian Muslims out of "their" part of Bosnia, they could claim it as their own. Bosnia would cease to exist and nationalist leaders could proclaim victory.

Yugoslavia was in Europe, and its people, however much they believed themselves divided, looked like Germans, French, or Americans. So reporters poured into Bosnia to report on the violence there.[37] What they found astonished them. Bosnian Serbs imprisoned Bosnian Muslims in concentration camps such as Jasenovac, where they were starved, raped, and worked to the point of death. Villages were burned, male leaders executed, and the survivors driven off. And Bosnian Serb forces, aided by forces from Serbia itself, encircled the capital city, Sarajevo, and besieged it for years. The human cost of the war was extraordinary. It's no wonder that Europeans—journalists, politicians, and ordinary people alike—were reminded of the Holocaust. And it's no wonder that the Security Council would begin to ask whether what was happening in Bosnia should be called genocide.

The Question of Intervention

It's likely the international community would not have intervened based solely on the human costs of this war. But Bosnia sits in the heart of eastern Europe. And by 1992 there was a universal perception that the collapse of Yugoslavia in general and the attack on Bosnia in particular threatened the national interests of the United States and many European countries. The danger was not economic (Yugoslavia had few natural resources worth mentioning), rather political and diplomatic. Southeastern Europe had been torn apart by the two world wars. Almost every country in this area nursed grievances stemming from the postwar treaties. Almost every nation hoped to reclaim what was rightfully theirs or were afraid their neighbors wanted to tear their country apart. If that happened, the Balkan countries wouldn't be the only casualties. The European Union (EU) might collapse as well.

The European Union was the end result of a long effort to integrate European countries politically and economically. Initially confined to western Europe (the EU originated with the Treaty of Rome of 1957, signed by France, England, West Germany, Belgium, Luxemburg, and the Netherlands), the community gradually expanded over the next decades. In the early 1990s, it was digesting the Treaty of Maastricht and the Schengen Agreement, which together eliminated passport checkpoints between (many) EU countries, opened the labor markets of individual countries to workers from anywhere in the EU, and most important, envisioned a common currency, the Euro. More to the point, with Soviet control over eastern Europe gone, the EU was contemplating expanding eastward. Throughout these changes ran two guiding motivations: the EU would strengthen Europe's economy vis-à-vis the United States and would, by tying countries together, keep the peace in a continent that had seen two devastating wars between 1914 and 1945.

Fighting in the Balkans had the potential to destroy not just plans for expansion but the whole EU structure itself. The collapse of Yugoslavia, leading to violence in Bosnia and imperiling stability in Albania and Macedonia, threatened to drag Greece (an EU member) into the conflict and could result in everyone's worst nightmare: clashes between Greece and Italy. Even if the EU could survive a war in Bosnia and the strain its numerous refugees were putting on Austria, Germany, and England, a general war in eastern Europe posed the very real threat of ending the EU altogether.

TIP

Many players are motivated by their perceived national interest. What national interests do the conflicts in Bosnia threaten? In Rwanda?

Accordingly, the United States and the EU quickly called on the UN to intervene. They did so speaking (and perhaps believing) the rhetoric of human rights. But in fact they were most interested in preserving national interests without sacrificing their political positions. Accordingly, both the UN and individual countries advocated for a limited intervention that would protect the population while they tried desperately to negotiate an end to the war. The UN Protection Force (UNPROFOR) was large, amounting to about 39,000 troops from about forty countries, but was hamstrung by the strict limitations of the Rules of Engagement and by cautious commanders.

Negotiations between the UN and the combatants repeatedly fell apart. As they did, the UN reluctantly expanded its mission in Bosnia. The Security Council added additional responsibilities to UNPROFOR four times in 1992–93, most significantly when it tasked UN forces with protecting designated safe areas around cities swarmed with refugees.

The result was the worst of all possible worlds: a UN intervention asked to protect civilians but limited in resources and unable to risk the political costs that would accompany casualties.[38] All sides in Bosnia quickly realized the constraints placed on UN forces and moved to take advantage of them. Television news showed footage of local commanders laughing at UN admonitions to stop abusing human rights. Bosnian Serbs stopped UN supply convoys on the road and prevented them from moving on until they provided arms and supplies to their captors. Both sides publicly ignored UN threats to use air or even ground power to intervene. By early 1994, UN leaders were spending much of their time thinking about, talking about, and worrying about the former Yugoslavia in general and Bosnia in particular.

CONCLUSION

For the most part, all this occurs in the background during the Rwandan game. In the context of the game, however, many leaders loyal to the United Nations and its ideals feel a pressing need to protect and enhance the organization's public image. This image is taking daily hits from events in Bosnia and elsewhere. The UN can't afford another catastrophe that turns public opinion even further against it. Even if you look toward Africa, you can't afford to ignore events in the rest of the world. If the UN collapses, all of you (well, almost all of you) lose.

KEY CONCEPTS AND TERMS

You'll need to understand and use several key terms while playing *The Needs of Others*. What follows is a brief introduction to three of them. These short discussions won't be sufficient—you'll need to spend time and energy applying the concepts to the situation in Rwanda and, perhaps, Bosnia. The following serves as a solid starting point.

Genocide

One issue central to the game is the definition and nature of the term *genocide*, coined by the Polish thinker and activist Raphael Lemkin in 1944. It entered the mainstream after the adoption of the UN Convention on the Prevention and Punishment of the Crime of Genocide (1948) and has since become widely used.

In popular discussion, the word *genocide* tends to be used broadly. Over the past half century, activists and reporters have applied the label to Bangladesh, Indonesia, Darfur, Cambodia, and other countries. It has been used metaphorically as well to characterize actions that threaten species at risk of extinction or military campaigns that threaten civilians. In that sense, the word functions in much the same way as the word *holocaust*—a quick label for something really bad.

For specialists and diplomats, defining genocide is much more problematic. The definition laid out in the UN Convention on the Prevention and Punishment of the Crime of Genocide is clearly the most influential. You'll read the convention in its entirety as part of your preparation for the game. For now, you can view the word *convention* as a synonym of *treaty*, an agreement between a number of countries to behave in a certain way. In this case, the convention lays out a single definition for what constitutes genocide and what countries are obliged to do should it occur. However, scholars point to several complications that emerge from the UN definition. Most obvious is the glaring omission of political groups from the list of possible victims. Given how often political conflicts drive human rights violations and how difficult it is to disentangle political from racial/religious identities, leaving political groups out of the convention significantly limits its applicability. Second, the phrase *in whole or in part*, while understandable and even necessary, is extraordinarily nebulous. How big of a group is necessary to invoke the convention? Half? A quarter? A few? One? Is the intentional targeting of one gender genocidal?[39] What exactly is the line that violators must not cross? Finally, scholars and others worry the vagueness of the definition conflates ethnic cleansing or targeted killings with genocide. Is ethnic cleansing—defined here as a policy of targeted killing and rape designed to frighten members of a group into leaving their land and thus opening up that land to settlement—genocidal? What about cultural genocide—roughly defined as the attempt to eradicate a group by destroying the habits, histories, traditions, and other things that bind members into a common community? Does the convention require the same response to a policy of forcing children to go to schools that teach different traditions from their native culture as it does to mass killings?[40]

Historically, signatory nations have hesitated or declined to invoke the Genocide Convention. For governments that do not want to intervene, the ambiguities and gaps in the convention provide ready-made opportunities to refuse to act.

Sovereignty

The game asks you to consider the nature of sovereignty in the modern world. In brief, *sovereignty* refers to the philosophical concept and legal reality that the government of a state has authority over everything that happens in that state. The state's governing documents may limit its powers. But its own citizens place these limitations on the government. Outside governments and individuals have no legal ability to force the state to do anything.

The idea of sovereignty is newer and its practice more limited than we often realize. In Europe, states shared power with religious institutions and with local and regional authorities for centuries. Only after the Peace of Westphalia in 1648 (the treaty that ended the Thirty Years' War) were princes (or leaders with other titles but similar roles) granted the exclusive right to make policies for the land and peoples under their control. In reality, states struggled well into the nineteenth century to limit or eliminate the role of local elites and clergy.

Outside of Europe, the concept of sovereignty was even more problematic. Consider East Asia, where China saw itself more as a big brother to Japan, Korea and other countries than it did a fellow state. In Africa, where underpopulation left vast areas without an effective government, disgruntled individuals could simply go off to the bush.

Nevertheless, by the late nineteenth century, increasingly successful imposition of central control within European states, the expansion of the European presence through imperialism, and the perceived need by many societies to adopt European ideas to escape European control created a widespread acceptance of the notion of sovereignty. Indeed, the reappearance of autarky (the policy goal of producing everything a state needed within its borders and thus, not needing to trade with another country for any essential good) as a national goal demonstrates how far governments believed sovereignty should extend. Respect for sovereignty was never universal, especially in religious traditions such as Christianity, which believed all Christians owed their allegiance first to the church and only then to their country. And even in the nineteenth century, organizations like the Red Cross tried to work within the constraints of sovereign nations to bring relief to the victims of conflicts. But the state was at its most powerful in the first half of the twentieth century.

As discussed earlier, the cataclysmic conflicts of the twentieth century called the wisdom of sovereignty into question. In addition to the League of Nations and the UN, a variety of nongovernmental organizations sprang up in the decades after World War II to critique the claims of nations to sovereignty. NGOs sought to alleviate poverty, aid victims of disasters, lobby for the rights of refugees, protect the environment, and monitor the compliance of governments with international agreements. Most important for this game, NGOs sent observers and reporters to publicize governments' mistreatment of their citizens (commonly referred to as "to name and to shame").

Nevertheless, by the 1990s, governments largely continued to monopolize the right to make decisions for their citizens. The increasingly intertwined nature of a globalizing world created significant legal checks to a state's power, but ones a state agreed to voluntarily. The same was true of international organizations like the UN, the General Agreement on Trade and Tariffs (the precursor to the World Trade Organization), and the European Union. An increasingly vocal minority of academics and civil society organizations critiqued sovereignty as an organizing principle. Nevertheless, sovereignty remained the philosophical foundation of the world order.

Human Rights

Finally, some background on human rights, a term that refers to the rights humans possess by virtue of their humanity rather than rights granted by treaty or citizenship in a state. Like sovereignty, the idea of human rights is relatively new. Universalist religious traditions such as Christianity and Islam have long asserted rights existed by virtue of one's identity as a child of God. But the power of religious institutions to enforce these ideas was limited and even these traditions often privileged members of the faith. Governments, by contrast, granted rights to their citizens. Such rights might be expansive or limited, but states guaranteed and enforced them. Because governments have the authority to enforce only their own laws in their own territory, no international legal system existed, and infractions on these rights could be punished only by force.

The idea that people possess rights by virtue of being born human has its origins in the eighteenth century. Why this occurred need not detain us here. Relevant for the game, however, is the gradual emergence of a body of thought about human rights and the demands such rights put on people and governments. In particular, a series of postconflict trials asserted both the existence of universal human rights and the legal authority of *any* state to enforce such rights and punish those who violate them. The first of these trials occurred after the Napoleonic conflicts of the early 1800s. The tactic then lay fallow for a century, to reemerge in the aftermath of World War I, when the victorious countries attempted to try both German and Ottoman officials for crimes against humanity (the latter for the ethnic cleansing and mass murder of Armenians, the former for atrocities against Belgian and French civilians, among other charges). Most famously, after World War II both the Soviet Union and the western allies put German and Japanese leaders on trial for violations of human rights. Most important in this process was the creation of a pair of tribunals to determine guilt or innocence and to administer justice. In Europe the trials were held at Nuremberg, in the Pacific at Tokyo. In both cases, judges heard testimony from victims, made legal rulings based on appeals from the lawyers for the defendants, and issued rulings on the guilt or innocence of the accused. In doing so, they formalized the notion of crimes against humanity.[41]

War crime tribunals then largely faded from the scene. Partly this was due to perceptions that the Nuremberg Trials had been unfair and unsuccessful. Moreover, the Cold War forestalled a consensus on which crimes should be tried and how to do so. Finally, states were unwilling to devote time, resources, and reputation for what they believed would be limited rewards.

The notion of universal human rights, however, was here to stay. What exactly these rights are remained highly contested. You'll be examining the "Universal Declaration of Human Rights," one example of a comprehensive attempt to identify what is meant by a *human right*. Philosophers, lawyers, and politicians have set to work to formulate other universal understandings of these rights and to create institutions to protect them.

None of these proposals has won universal support. Similarly, the question of how to enforce human rights remains controversial. Nevertheless, most people (if not most governments) acknowledge that humans have rights by virtue of being alive and that governments should protect these rights. And people continue to invoke the notion of human rights and to call on others to defend them.

 PART 3: THE GAME

MAJOR ISSUES FOR DEBATE

During the game, you will debate three different sets of issues.

The first set involves the factual and definitional. What is happening in Rwanda? Who is to blame? And what is the right word to express what is happening? Answering these questions is surprisingly difficult. Getting information from a place far away in a world before Twitter, Facebook, and GPS is hard. Agreeing on what that information means is even more challenging.

The second revolves around what you should do with this information. Put differently, your discussions will ask what you should or may do to alleviate human suffering in Rwanda. May the UN authorize armed intervention in Rwanda? Under what conditions? With what limitations? For what goals? For how long? These questions are both philosophical and legal. Rwanda is a sovereign state, a member of the UN. The UN's powers and responsibilities toward its member states are well articulated in its Charter as well as in specific treaties and conventions. These legal documents may or may not accord with your sense of what needs to be done.

Finally, there are also practical questions. What can you do with the resources available to you? How many troops can you find? Who will pay them? How long will they be available to you? And is there a way to use them effectively? Perhaps most important, is there a way to intervene without risking significant UN casualties or without getting sucked into a long-term, costly intervention?

As you play the game and debate these questions, you'll be looking at a specific application of broader questions. As such, by the end of the game you will have a deeper understanding of the following:

- The basic debates regarding human rights and the role of states in a global world.

- The role and functions of the United Nations and various other international or transnational organizations.

- The historical background, course, and consequences of events in Rwanda in 1994.

- The intersection of domestic politics, the media, public opinion, and international and transnational organizations.

- The complexities of making decisions and policy in an environment with inadequate and unequal access to information.

- Leadership, negotiation, and critical thinking.

- Speaking and writing critically and persuasively.

RULES AND PROCEDURES

Objectives and Victory Conditions

Players' objectives in *The Needs of Others* revolve around the question of stopping the violence in Rwanda. Some players will win by limiting the UN response, others by authorizing and implementing a response that stops the violence or at least protects civilians from harm. In this sense, the game is simple. However, there are a couple points that need to be emphasized.

First, the game is not over until the last round is complete. Decisions made in one round can be overridden or changed in a subsequent meeting. The GM will decide who won or lost *after* the game, not during it.

Second, the question of saving civilians is a complicated one. Simply ordering an intervention is not sufficient to stop the violence. Effective intervention depends on the size of the force, the nature of the intervention, the rules governing how the intervention force operates, the geography of the region in which you are intervening, and the politics of the conflict. In a short game (which *The Needs of Others* is, even though it may seem long to you in the context of a traditional class), you will not have the ability to examine these issues in the same detail that the UN would in real life. However, you'll need to address them as deeply as you are able in the time available to you (which won't be much).

If, at the end of the game, there is no UN force in Rwanda, the GM will announce who has won and who has lost. But if UN troops (or troops from a UN member state) are in Rwanda, either as part of UNAMIR or as part of a new UN force, the GM will roll a die to determine the result of this intervention, including the number of casualties the UN force takes.

That some victories will be determined by the roll of a die may seem unfair or capricious. It is not. Interventions are always fraught with dangers and surprises. Decisions by force commanders, negotiations between combatants, and actions of individual soldiers can impact global affairs disproportionately. Put more simply, whether an intervention is successful depends on luck as well as skill.

But factors such as the degree of preparation for a mission, the balance of forces in a conflict, and the willingness of public opinion to accept casualties also affect the likelihood of success. As such, each die roll is heavily weighted by events or choices made during the game. You can't control the outcome. But you can maximize the chances for success by careful preparation.

Terminology

The game book and your individual role sheets employ a standard terminology regarding the game. Each *round* contains one *meeting* of the UNSC and one *set* of press conferences.

BASIC OUTLINE OF THE GAME

The game proceeds in a series of rounds. The length of each round and its parts depends on the format of the class (two times per week, three times per week, etc.). Ordinarily there are five rounds in a game. These rounds occur on the following dates during the crisis of 1994. All dates and times are Eastern Time (New York City).

TIP

Be sure to ask the GM about any modifications to the rules and procedures as laid out in this game book.

- Round 1: April 7, 9:00 A.M.

- Round 2: April 15, 12:00 noon

- Round 3: April 30, 12:00 noon

- Round 4: May 15, 12:00 noon

- Round 5: May 30, 12:00 noon

Each round (except the last) consists of two parts.

Meetings of the UN Security Council

The UNSC meetings are where decisions are made. Players may present papers, introduce proposals, ask questions, request reports or information (from the secretary-general, for instance), or act in other ways. Many players will make formal speeches at these meetings. For most of the game, however, informal debate will be the norm.

The chairperson of these meetings rotates among the UNSC members. For game sessions that occur in April (the first three rounds of the game) the chair is the ambassador of New Zealand. In May (the final two rounds) the chair is the ambassador of Nigeria. It is the chair's responsibility to construct agendas, run meetings, and ensure orderly debates and decisions.

During these sessions, ambassadors who represent member states sitting on the UNSC may raise whatever issues or concerns they have about international issues. Typically, sessions will open with a few set-piece speeches, following which the chair will invite comments or proposals.

Players not represented on the UNSC may (and will) attend these meetings (sitting somewhere in the back of the room away from the conference table). They may raise questions or make presentations if allowed to by the chair of the Security Council. However, they have no legal right to make their opinions heard and the chair may order them to be quiet during sessions. The chair *must* allow students required to make formal speeches to present these to the UNSC.

Should the UNSC members wish, they may meet in private sessions. Such a private session is limited to 20 minutes (and must be wholly contained in one class period). **The UNSC may hold only two such private sessions in the course of the game. Neither private session may occur during the fifth round of the game.** During a private session, other players must leave the classroom (but must return when the public session reconvenes—this is not a chance to leave class early). The UNSC may not take any official action during a private session (there may certainly be straw polls, but any decision must have a public, on-the-record vote before it becomes effective). The purpose of a private session is usually to allow players to speak frankly without the media or public opinion present. Remember, however, that Journalists may later ask about the private session.

The UN secretary-general attends all Security Council meetings and should participate in its debates. The secretary-general does *not*, however, have a vote. This person may be asked to provide reports, suggestions, or other guidance at the discretion of the UNSC. The Gamemaster may choose to limit the number or length of such reports to ensure an appropriate workload for the secretary-general.

Motions and Voting

- Any player with a seat on the UNSC may put forward a formal proposal (for instance, "I propose we end the mandate for UNAMIR and withdraw UNAMIR forces immediately"). After such a motion, the chair is required to allow discussion and proposals for amendments. Motions (or amendments to the motion) pass if they receive the votes of 60 percent of the members of the Security Council (for a game with five Security Council members, 3 votes are needed; for six members, 4 votes; for seven members, 5 votes; and so on). **However, if *any* permanent member of the Security Council votes *against* a proposal, it automatically fails, even if every other member of the council votes to approve it.** The permanent powers are the United States, Great Britain, France, China, and Russia.

- In certain situations, Representatives of Public Opinion may attempt to force their ambassador to vote in a particular way. The mechanics of this are laid out in the relevant role sheets, but note that the chair will pause for thirty seconds or so before asking for a vote to allow Representatives of Public Opinion a chance to intervene.

- If the chair of the UNSC believes sufficient time has been allotted for discussion, he or she may call for a vote. "Bob's Rules of Order" (p. 147 in this game book) addresses how this works. The GM may intervene at any time to prevent excessive stalling or rushing to votes.

The culture of the UNSC is one of formality and politeness. While there is no obligation to re-create the manners and expectations of the UNSC completely, one element of this culture is required. All members of the UNSC (or people who speak in front of the UNSC) are required to dress in business casual or more formally.

Press Conferences

During the second phase of each round, players other than Journalists are able to hold press conferences. The purpose is to present their views to the Journalists and others and to answer questions.

At the end of each UNSC session (except the final UNSC meeting), the GM will ask who will be holding a press conference and where they will gather. Players wanting to do so should announce that they will hold a press conference. There will then be a short pause (one to two minutes, no more) to plan. Following the pause, players holding press conferences will go to their designated space, make an opening statement (this need not be long), and answer questions. Players may also choose to distribute press releases to those attending the conference. Conceivably, they may limit a press conference to such prepared statements. Ordinarily, however, Journalists and others will be allowed and encouraged to ask questions. The representative of the UNSC *must* allow this question period. Once all questions have been answered (or evaded) or the class period ends, the press conference is over.

The UNSC is required to hold a press conference in each round except the May 30 session. The chair must be present. One or two ambassadors may join the chair. Journalists or other non-UNSC representatives may ask for specific ambassadors to be present. Such requests may be accepted or rejected, but players should keep in mind the public relations impact of refusing to answer questions from the media. To keep conferences manageable, it is preferable that no more than three representatives be present at any one press conference.

Other organizations or individuals may announce they will hold press conferences as they wish. Press conferences occur simultaneously (in different parts of the room), thus each player may participate in only one press conference at a time. Any organization or individual holding a press conference *must* announce that fact and the location of the press conference. The conferences should be held far enough apart that noise from one will not disturb another. If necessary, press conferences may be held in the hall outside the classroom or similar locations.

Press conferences function as venues in which the players who are off stage during UNSC meetings take a central role. Accordingly, Journalists, members of NGOs, and Representatives of Public Opinion have priority in terms of asking questions. If time allows, UNSC ambassadors may ask questions as well.

Press conferences exist for a purpose. For those answering questions, press conferences are an opportunity to present their positions persuasively. For Journalists and others asking questions, these conferences are at least an opportunity to acquire information but often are also a chance to persuade (by forcing ambassadors to provide information they'd rather withhold, by leading ambassadors to present their arguments in a different way, etc.). They are a critical part of the game and require as much forethought and care as do UNSC debates. Players should not see them as an opportunity to leave class early (and the GM will undoubtedly severely penalize your participation grade if you do).

Press conferences function as something like a free market of ideas. People not presenting at press conferences may move from one to the other as they wish. Organizations trying to get the attention of the media are competing with each other for their attention. If no one attends your press conference (or if they leave early or ignore what is being said), you miss the chance to persuade those yet undecided.

Press conferences are *not* opportunities for UNSC ambassadors to continue debate. They exist for Journalists and other players (Representatives of Public Opinion, members of NGOs, etc.) to ask questions of policy makers. The Gamemaster will intervene if ambassadors use this as an opportunity to argue with each other.

It's likely that you've never actually seen a press conference, or that you've seen only clips of one on a news or sports station. If you're not sure of the appropriate voice or tone to use, or you just want to see one in action, you can find transcripts of press conferences hosted by Ban Ki-moon, the secretary-general of the UN in 2016, at www.un.org/press/en/content/secretary-general/press-conference and video of recent White House press conferences at www.youtube.com/user /whitehouse.

Demonstrations

- People who feel excluded from or ignored at formal sites of debate and discussion often resort to unauthorized demonstrations or other kinds of protest to make their feelings known. Demonstrations in *The Lives of Others* play the same role. They allow players who feel they are being silenced or that their opinions are not being heard to have a voice. They are an extremely powerful way to convey opposition or disgust.

- These demonstrations are often more emotional, more inclusive, and less routinized. That does not mean, however, they don't have their own distinctive grammar, strategies, and practices. Accordingly, players planning demonstrations should consider the ways demonstrations are traditionally structured and follow these principles. Demonstrations are not the place to make long, rational (boring?) speeches—they are places to use call and response, to sing songs or perform chants, to wave signs and placards, to wear specific colors of T-shirts or body art, etc. In particular, images are often more effective than words.

- Players may demonstrate during actual meetings of the UNSC. However, the chair may direct the police (the Gamemaster) to eject demonstrators from the room if they refuse to follow the chair's directions. This is the extent of the chair's powers—the chair may not throw people in jail or banish them from the country.

- Demonstrations held before or after a UNSC meeting itself may *not* be stopped. For example, demonstrations in the hallways outside of the classroom or that break out after the official closing of the meeting— metaphorically speaking, as the representatives leave the building— may be held without consequence. The Gamemaster will determine how long such demonstrations are allowed to continue before returning to other game activities.

- Individuals or organizations (including Representatives of Public Opinion) may also demonstrate during press conferences. The Gamemaster will determine how long to allow such demonstrations to continue before returning to the press conference. Demonstrations are not always received favorably by public opinion but may in some cases be the only way to get your views across.

Other Considerations

- The Gamemaster will periodically advance the action by distributing bulletins containing news of historical events. Some of these bulletins will be public (available to everyone). Others will be distributed to specific factions/players for use as they see fit.

- Players may find it wise to distribute messages, petitions, or other writings to a specific individual player or to all other players as a group throughout the game in addition to their assigned papers. These will not receive formal grades, but do count for class participation, so make sure the instructor gets a copy of whatever you distribute. If you wish to distribute something anonymously, contact the Gamemaster, who will assist you in this.

- This game deals with events and issues that can evoke powerful emotions and reactions. Players may find themselves raising their voices, slamming the table, or using language not normally allowed in the classroom. Reacting that way during the game is reasonable and appropriate. Urgency, frustration, and anger are acceptable emotions to present in class. If you do so, remember two things. First, you are trying to persuade other people to act a certain way. Emotional behavior or reactions are sometimes useful in this attempt but sometimes damaging. Second, as you confront or accuse, remember you are doing so to the other players' *roles* not to the students themselves. After the game is over, your role disappears, but your relationship with your fellow students will not. *Always be careful to separate the one from the other.*

OUTSIDE RESEARCH: ESPECIALLY IMPORTANT

Events in *The Needs of Others* move quickly, and rounds of the game are closely spaced chronologically. Students are encouraged to do outside reading to supplement their understanding of the material. **However, students may not refer to events or introduce pieces of information before they occurred or before knowledge of them were received in real life.** For example, if it happened on April 16, it *cannot* be used in the game session that takes place on April 15.

In the same way, players may not introduce information unavailable to them in real life. For instance, UNAMIR communications were directed specifically along the UN chain of command and would not be available to non-UN personnel (or even to UN ambassadors). If you can prove the information you've uncovered would have been available to your character in real life, it can be used. **If you aren't sure, ask the Gamemaster before you mention it in the game.**

GAME VERSIONS AND SESSIONS

Three versions of *The Needs of Others* game are presented here. Your instructor will tell you which version you are playing and whether there will be any modifications to the schedule as given here.

TABLE 1

Standard Version

CLASS SESSION	SCHEDULED ACTIVITY	STUDENT RESPONSIBILITY	DATE OF GAME PLAY	SESSION LEADER
1	Introduction to Reacting and to the game	Read parts 1, 3, and 4 of the game book	N/A	GM
2	Introduction to the UN and Rwanda	Read Part 2 of the game book and the core texts on pp. 76–146	N/A	GM
3	Introduction to theories of humanitarian intervention	Read the core texts on pp. 76–146	N/A	GM
4	Round 1	UNSC meeting and press conferences	April 7	Ambassador from New Zealand
5	Round 2	UNSC meeting and press conferences	April 15	Ambassador from New Zealand
6	Round 3	UNSC meeting and press conferences	April 30	Ambassador from New Zealand
7	Round 4	UNSC meeting and press conferences	May 15	Ambassador from Nigeria
8	Round 5 and begin postmortem	UNSC meeting; discussion of game and what really happened (GM may announce winners and losers)	May 30	Ambassador from Nigeria and GM
9	Postmortem concluded	Discuss game and what really happened (GM announces winners and losers)	N/A	GM

TABLE 2

Extended Version

CLASS SESSION	SCHEDULED ACTIVITY	STUDENT RESPONSIBILITY	DATE OF GAME PLAY	SESSION LEADER
1	Introduction to Reacting and to the game	Read Parts 1, 3, and 4 of the game book	N/A	GM
2	Introduction to the UN and Rwanda	Read Part 2 of the game book, the UN Charter (available online), and the Convention on the Prevention and Punishment of the Crime of Genocide (see p. 82)	N/A	GM
3	Introduction to theories of humanitarian intervention	Read the remaining material in the game book	N/A	GM
4	Finish introduction	*Everyone:* plan strategy; *American faction:* meet, and if there is more than one American player, their **papers are due today**	N/A	GM
5	Round 1	UNSC meeting and press conferences	April 7	Ambassador from New Zealand
6	Round 2	UNSC meeting and press conferences	April 15	Ambassador from New Zealand
7	Round 3	UNSC meeting and press conferences	April 30	Ambassador from New Zealand
8	Round 4	UNSC meeting and press conferences	May 15	Ambassador from Nigeria
9	Round 5 and begin postmortem	UNSC meeting; discussion of game and what really happened (GM may announce winners and losers)	May 30	Ambassador from Nigeria and GM
10	Postmortem concluded	Discuss game and what really happened (GM announces winners and losers)	N/A	GM

TABLE 3

Compressed Version

CLASS SESSION	SCHEDULED ACTIVITY	STUDENT RESPONSIBILITY	DATE OF GAME PLAY	SESSION LEADER
1	Introduction to Reacting and the game	Read game book, pp. 2–11	N/A	GM
2	Introduction to the UN and Rwanda	Read game book, pp. 12–55	N/A	GM
3	Round 1	UNSC meeting and press conferences	April 15	Ambassador from New Zealand
4	Round 2	UNSC meeting and press conferences	April 30	Ambassador from New Zealand
5	Round 3	UNSC meeting and press conferences	May 15	Ambassador from Nigeria
6	Round 4	UNSC meeting; discussion of game and what really happened (GM may announce winners and losers)	May 30	Ambassador from Nigeria and GM
7 (optional)	Postmortem	Discuss game and what really happened (GM announces winners and losers)	N/A	GM

ASSIGNMENTS

Ordinarily each player will write two formal papers. These papers should be **four to five pages** long. The Gamemaster may alter this length or the number of assigned papers. The topics for your papers are listed in your role sheet.

Most players will present their first paper formally to the UNSC. The GM will work with the ambassador from New Zealand to set guidelines for this speech. Keep the following points in mind:

- You may *not* read your speech. You may work from prepared notes.

- You should be prepared to answer questions about your speech.

- You can assume you will not have enough time to present all the information in your paper. Thus your speech will be different from your paper, although based on it.

- You should provide the other players with a copy of any paper you plan to present to the UNSC; distribution should take place several hours before that session (the GM will identify the precise time and way to do this).

WARNING ! *In the extended version of the game, papers from American policy makers are due before the game starts. (Ask your GM for instructions.)*

Some players may choose to structure their second paper in the form of a letter to a specific player or as a newspaper article. Ask the GM how to submit these papers, especially if you want them to remain secret from some players.

 PART 4: ROLES AND FACTIONS

Before the game begins, you'll be assigned a role in one of five groups, either as a UN ambassador, a government official, a representative of a human rights organization, a Journalist, or a Representative of Public Opinion. While the number of players in each category depends on class size, at least one role from each group will be present. Each role has specific, publicly acknowledged responsibilities during the game. Each has general stances on humanitarian issues, which can be inferred from the person's title and past actions. You'll be given a role sheet that details the individual you're playing as well as specific instructions and requirements for winning (victory conditions). Information in your role sheet is *known only to you*.

In large classes, more than one player will represent a single country on the UNSC. Most of the time, however, you'll be on your own. Still, there are almost always other players who share your views. It is wise to seek these players out and share ideas and plan strategy. There is no prohibition against such informal factions in the game.

Regardless of any alliances you make, **do not show your role sheet to another player.** It is at one and the same time your mission and your identity. You could no more share all of yourself with another person than you could fully understand someone else. You may, as you choose, share information from that sheet verbally. If another player opens up to you, you must decide whether to trust the disclosure, to treat it with suspicion, or to dismiss it as disinformation or falsification. In the game, as in life, there is no formal penalty for lying. If someone offers to show you his or her role sheet, be cautious. That individual may have a falsified role sheet or otherwise may be trying to mislead you.

UN Ambassadors and Advisers

The players on the UNSC have the (ahistorical) responsibility for formulating national policy and advocating for that policy in the council. The game frequently gives a country's ambassadors the right to make policy rather than simply represent it. Depending on class size, some ambassadors may be advised by staff members representing specific interests in their government. It is the responsibility of the ambassadors to argue in the UN for their desired outcome and to vote on UNSC proposals. They are also responsible for meeting with the press during press conferences. Some ambassadors and staff have specific policy outcomes dictated by their victory conditions. Others are Indeterminates, players initially undecided about the issues. Their votes will depend on how effective other players are at convincing them. Unlike other Reacting games, Indeterminates are not publicly identified; these players may, however, reveal their status to other players if they wish.

UN and U.S. Officials

Some players have specific roles and motivations in connection to the UNSC. Every game will include Secretary-General Boutros Boutros-Ghali. The presence of other roles depends on class size.

Representatives of Human Rights Organizations and other NGOs

Nongovernmental Organizations (NGOs) such as the International Committee of the Red Cross (ICRC), the Heritage Foundation, and Human Rights Watch (HRW) played an increasingly important role in reporting on and lobbying against human rights abuses in the 1980s and 1990s. Players representing these organizations must persuade the UNSC to implement their desired agenda. Generally, they will not play an active role during UNSC sessions. Instead, they must make their case in public (via news conferences, press releases, and demonstrations) and through private lobbying.

Journalists

Both television and print media inform the public about international affairs. In theory and oftentimes in practice, they do this through a combination of reporting from crisis areas, from national capitals, and from the UN. Because of Rwanda's remoteness and the limited resources available to news organizations, few Journalists in the game are able to spend significant time on the ground in Rwanda itself. Most will learn about events by covering debates in the UN or among national policy makers and by interviewing human rights experts and lobby groups. In the game, Journalists produce newspapers (or, for those technologically sophisticated students, audio or visual reports) read by policy makers and the public. Journalists will listen to UNSC debates and will use press conferences as opportunities to question policy makers and other players. While some Journalists may take brief trips to Rwanda, most will be present throughout the game. Because public opinion is critical in democratic politics, and because Journalists often play a significant role in swaying public opinion, the quality and direction of the Journalists' writings can be vital in shaping national policy.

Representatives of Public Opinion

Representatives of the public are initially Indeterminates; they are politically interested but unelected citizens of various countries. Their role is to listen carefully throughout the game and decide which side is most convincing. These players serve as a proxy for the public opinion polling and electoral dynamics that shape policy in a democracy. Certain players must secure the support (or at least indifference) of public opinion to win the game. Others may be forced to align their own policy with that demanded by public opinion. Accordingly, players given this role *must* listen carefully to the public discussion but *must also* be careful consumers of the newspapers and reporting (which may contain information not made public in the UNSC debates or press conferences) and be open to meeting with other players privately.

Possible Roles

UN AMBASSADORS AND ADVISERS

United States	Nigeria
The United Kingdom	Pakistan
France	Oman
China	Djibouti
Russia	Argentina
New Zealand	Brazil
Czech Republic	Indonesia
Spain	

Descriptions of Select Roles

UN AND U.S. OFFICIALS

Boutros Boutros-Ghali: Secretary-general of the United Nations. Taught international law and politics for twenty-eight years before becoming foreign minister of Egypt. Became secret ary-general in 1991. Author of the UN policy document "An Agenda for Peace."

Anthony Lake: U.S. national security adviser, appointed by President Bill Clinton. Long-time member of the American foreign policy elite. Among other projects, has commissioned a re-examination of America's role in peacekeeping operations in the wake of Somalia.

Donald Brewer: Colonel in the U.S. Army. A Vietnam War veteran who has served in army planning positions since late 1980s.

Prudence Bushnell: U.S. State Department official who has served in residence in Africa and has helped develop policy positions in Washington.

REPRESENTATIVES OF HUMAN RIGHTS ORGANIZATIONS

Alison Des Forges: Senior member of Human Rights Watch who has a PhD in African history from Yale University. Although she teaches full-time at the university level, she spends much time as a traveling representative of HRW.

Gerard Belengar: Senior official of the International Committee of the Red Cross. Born in Switzerland, he has lived in several countries and has served in the Red Cross most of his professional life.

Daryl Thompson: Official in the Heritage Foundation who has a law degree from Georgetown University. Has moved between academia and policy positions since graduation.

JOURNALISTS

Pete Danell: A long-time journalist who has been covering politics and foreign affairs since the 1960s. Although not nationally famous, he is widely respected in the field.

Quinn Bonham: Recently received a master's degree in journalism and now works for the Associated Press. Has written a variety of stories on subjects of limited public interest. Now he covers Africa for the AP.

Kelli Harper: Long-time journalist with a master's degree from the University of Michigan. She spent years covering local- and then state-level politics before moving to foreign affairs; she now writes for the *Wall Street Journal*.

 PART 5: CORE TEXTS

BRIEF INTRODUCTION TO THE READING

There are four kinds of texts in *The Needs of Others*. Some are included in this game book; you'll find others online or in your school's library. In the following section you'll find questions to keep in mind as you read the documents required for every player.

The first group of core texts consists of several UN documents. The first is excerpts from the UN Charter, which is *not included in this game book*, but is readily available online. The foundational document of the United Nations, the charter lays out the vision for the organization, what it is supposed to accomplish, and what it can and can't do in pursuit of these goals.

You need not read the entire Charter. Rather, you should read the following sections:

Preamble

Chapter 1: Article 1; Article 2, paragraphs 1, 4, and 7

Chapter 5: Article 24, paragraphs 1 and 2

Chapter 6: Articles 33–38

Chapter 7: Articles 39–45

All players should read two additional UN documents, referred to as covenants or conventions. These are agreements ratified by most member nations of the UN that modify or elaborate on the Charter. Each is important, but each functions differently. The Convention on the Prevention and Punishment of the Crime of Genocide is reprinted in the game book; the "Universal Declaration of Human Rights" is readily available online.

Finally, there are heavily edited excerpts of two resolutions (Resolution 872 and Resolution 909, both in the game book) passed by the UNSC to establish and regulate the United Nations Assistance Mission in Rwanda. They are important aids to understanding what the UNSC wanted to do in the country and what limits it established for its assistance.

The second category of core texts consists of chapters or articles reprinted from other texts that lay out views on humanitarian intervention. They are written by philosophers and academics. This makes for reading that is sometimes dense. You will have to pay careful attention to the ideas and the chain of reasoning the authors lay out. By doing so, you'll be rewarded with a pretty thorough sense of what people were thinking in the years before the game begins. I chose them not only because of their intellectual richness but because they represent widely understood and discussed approaches to a complicated problem. Politicians may not have read these (in fact, they almost certainly didn't), but they would have been familiar with the ideas presented in the documents.

The third category of core text consists of speeches and reports made by politicians. Several of these are reprinted in the game book. They are often fairly straightforward. Nevertheless, you should read them carefully and completely.

The final category of core texts are in addition to the required reading that will help you play the game. Many players will benefit from a deeper knowledge about the Rwandan crisis. A number of role sheets suggest specific sources to consult, which will make playing those roles easier. If your role sheet doesn't include suggested reading, consult the Selected Bibliography (p. 150) or your instructor for ideas. Remember, however, that books or articles published *after* the Rwandan crisis are influenced by what happened. You may not be allowed to use all of this material because you would not have access to it in 1994.

QUESTIONS TO CONSIDER WHILE READING

Your instructor may use a variety of approaches to introducing the readings and history necessary to playing the game. However, as you prepare, you might consider using the following questions as a study guide.

UN Charter (available online)

- Why was the UN created and what vision did its creators have for the organization? How is this vision written into the Charter?

- According to this document, when and how can the UN intervene in conflict? When is it prohibited from doing so?

- *Pay close attention* to the following sections:
  - The Preamble

  - Chapter 1, Article 1 (especially paragraph 1) and Article 2 (especially paragraph 7)

  - Chapter 6, Articles 33–38

  - Chapter 7, Articles 39–45

Convention on the Prevention and Punishment of the Crime of Genocide

- Why was this convention created?

- How does this document define genocide? Are there any groups missing from this definition?

- How is a genocide declared? What obligations exist for signatories when such a declaration is made?

Resolutions 872 (1993) and 909 (1994) of the Security Council

- According to Resolution 872, what was UNAMIR's task in Rwanda? How might you know if it had been successful? How does Resolution 909 reflect the growing doubts of some members of the Security Council about UNAMIR's role?

"Universal Declaration of Human Rights" (available online)

- What kinds of rights are identified as such by the declaration? How do these differ from the rights identified in the U.S. Bill of Rights?

- Where do the identified rights come from (in other words, what is the philosophical basis for claiming these rights)?

- How is this declaration to be enforced?

- To what extent, if at all, does this declaration supersede the Convention on Genocide?

A Short History of Rwanda

- What impact did Belgian rule have on Rwanda?

- Define what it means to be a Hutu and a Tutsi. How has this meaning changed over time?

- How have Hutus and Tutsis interacted politically over time?

- How and why did the stability of Rwanda under Habyarimana decay and why is that important for Rwandan history?

- What role did Burundi and Uganda play in the history of Rwanda from 1961 to 1993?

The United Nations: A Brief History

- Why did world leaders decide an international organization was necessary in the aftermath of World War I? Why did this fail?

- Why try again after World War II?

- What were some of the ways that the Cold War impacted the shape and actions of the UN?

- How did the end of the Cold War change UN attitudes and behaviors?

- How did events in Somalia change UN perspectives on humanitarian intervention? Why?

- How and why did the UN get involved in Rwanda? What was its mission there? How did it try to achieve it?

Michael Walzer: *Just and Unjust Wars*

- Where do the rights of political communities come from?

- Why is aggression wrong in an international environment defined this way?

- What is the legalist paradigm?

- What guidelines does Walzer lay out for deciding when intervention into another state's business is appropriate?

- Why does he argue that intervening in another state to save its people from a domestic dictatorship (that is not committing atrocities) is wrong?

- What are the three possible exceptions to the general rule of nonintervention and how do they work?

Fernando Teson, *Humanitarian Intervention*

- Where do the rights of political communities come from?

- How does Teson compare to Walzer? Does Teson's definition make humanitarian intervention more plausible or less?

- What are the conditions that make humanitarian intervention admissible?

- What questions do countries need to ask themselves before adopting a policy of humanitarian intervention?

George H. W. Bush, "New World Order"

- Why is this speech generally referred to as the "New World Order" speech?

- How does Bush imagine the postwar world will work?

- What role should the United States play in this world? The UN?

François Mitterrand, Speech at La Baule

- What is Mitterrand's vision for the relationship between France and its African friends?

- How has history left these countries with significant challenges?

- What should be France's role in helping them?

Boutros Boutros-Ghali, "An Agenda for Peace"

- What role should the UN play in the new world as envisioned in this document?

- How might it go about doing that?

- How should the UN interact with sovereign states in carrying out this vision?

American Leadership Confronting the Challenges of a Broader World

- What problems do Bill Clinton and Madeleine Albright identify?

- How do they propose to solve these problems?

- What might happen if the changes Clinton and Albright envision don't occur?

American Responses to Mogadishu

- In what ways does Jesse Helms criticize Bill Clinton's foreign policy? Why does he include the UN in this criticism?

- What outcome would Helms like to see?

- How does Clinton defend his own actions? What policy does he want the United States to pursue after Mogadishu?

- How does Clinton present the relationship between the United States and the UN?

UNITED NATIONS GENERAL ASSEMBLY

Convention on the Prevention and Punishment of the Crime of Genocide

Adopted as Resolution 260 (III) A of the United Nations General Assembly on December 9, 1948. Questions to consider while reading: Why was this convention created? How does this document define genocide? Are there any groups missing from this definition? How is a genocide declared? What obligations exist for signatories when such a declaration is made?

ARTICLE 1

he Contracting Parties confirm that genocide, whether committed in time of peace or in time of war, is a crime under international law which they undertake to prevent and to punish.

ARTICLE 2

n the present Convention, genocide means any of the following acts committed with intent to destroy, in whole or in part, a national, ethnical, racial or religious group, as such:

(a) Killing members of the group;

(b) Causing serious bodily or mental harm to members of the group;

(c) Deliberately inflicting on the group conditions of life calculated to bring about its physical destruction in whole or in part;

(d) Imposing measures intended to prevent births within the group;

(e) Forcibly transferring children of the group to another group.

ARTICLE 3

he following acts shall be punishable:

(a) Genocide;

(b) Conspiracy to commit genocide;

(c) Direct and public incitement to commit genocide;

(d) Attempt to commit genocide;

(e) Complicity in genocide.

ARTICLE 4

ersons committing genocide or any of the other acts enumerated in Article 3 shall be punished, whether they are constitutionally responsible rulers, public officials or private individuals.

ARTICLE 5

he Contracting Parties undertake to enact, in accordance with their respective Constitutions, the necessary legislation to give effect to the provisions of the present Convention and, in particular, to provide effective penalties for persons guilty of genocide or any of the other acts enumerated in Article 3.

ARTICLE 6

Persons charged with genocide or any of the other acts enumerated in Article 3 shall be tried by a competent tribunal of the State in the territory of which the act was committed, or by such international penal tribunal as may have jurisdiction with respect to those Contracting Parties which shall have accepted its jurisdiction.

ARTICLE 7

Genocide and the other acts enumerated in Article 3 shall not be considered as political crimes for the purpose of extradition.

The Contracting Parties pledge themselves in such cases to grant extradition in accordance with their laws and treaties in force.

ARTICLE 8

Any Contracting Party may call upon the competent organs of the United Nations to take such action under the Charter of the United Nations as they consider appropriate for the prevention and suppression of acts of genocide or any of the other acts enumerated in Article 3.

* * *

UNITED NATIONS MEMBER COUNTRIES

Resolution 872 Establishes UNAMIR, 1993

In Resolutions 872 and 909, the UN Security Council first established, then extended, UNAMIR and its mandate in Rwanda. These resolutions lay out the reasons the Security Council believed UNAMIR necessary, what it was to do, and how it was to do it. According to Resolution 872, what was UNAMIR's task in Rwanda? How might you know if it had been successful? How does Resolution 909 reflect the growing doubts of some members of the Security Council about UNAMIR's role?

UN Security Council, Resolution 872 (1993), adopted by the Security Council at its 3288th meeting, on October 5, 1993, S/RES/872 (1993), www.unhcr.org/refworld/docid/3b00f16a8.html.

The Security Council,

Welcoming the signing of the Arusha Peace Agreement (including its Protocols) on 4 August 1993 and *urging* the parties to continue to comply fully with it,

* * *

Stressing the urgency of the deployment of an international neutral force in Rwanda, as underlined both by the Government of the Republic of Rwanda and by the Rwandese Patriotic Front and as reaffirmed by their joint delegation in New York,

* * *

Resolved that the United Nations should, at the request of the parties, and under peaceful conditions with the full cooperation of all the parties, make its full contribution to the implementation of the Arusha Peace Agreement,

* * *

2. *Decides* to establish a peace-keeping operation under the name United Nations Assistance Mission for Rwanda (UNAMIR) for a period of six months subject to the proviso that it will be extended beyond the initial ninety days only upon a review by the Council based on a report from the Secretary-General as to whether or not substantive progress has been made towards the implementation of the Arusha Peace Agreement;

3. *Decides* that drawing from the Secretary-General's recommendations, UNAMIR shall have the following mandate:

(a) To contribute to the security of the city of Kigali, inter alia, within a weapons secure area established by the parties in and around the city;

(b) To monitor observance of the cease-fire agreement, which calls for the establishment of cantonment and assembly zones and the demarcation of the new demilitarized zone and other demilitarization procedures;

(c) To monitor the security situation during the final period of the transitional government's mandate, leading up to the elections;

(d) To assist with mine clearance, primarily through training programmes;

(e) To investigate at the request of the parties or on its own initiative instances of alleged non-compliance with the provisions of the Arusha Peace Agreement relating to the integration of the armed forces, and pursue any such instances with the parties responsible and report thereon as appropriate to the Secretary-General;

(f) To monitor the process of repatriation of Rwandese refugees and resettlement of displaced persons to verify that it is carried out in a safe and orderly manner;

(g) To assist in the coordination of humanitarian assistance activities in conjunction with relief operations;

(h) To investigate and report on incidents regarding the activities of the gendarmerie and police;

* * *

9. *Invites* the Secretary-General to consider ways of reducing the total maximum strength of UNAMIR, in particular, through phased deployment without thereby affecting the capacity of UNAMIR to carry out its mandate and *requests* the Secretary-General in planning and executing the phased deployment of UNAMIR to seek economies and to report regularly on what is achieved in this regard.

* * *

11. *Urges* the parties to implement the Arusha Peace Agreement in good faith;

* * *

14. *Urges* Member States, United Nations agencies and non-governmental organizations to provide and intensify their economic, financial and humanitarian assistance in favour of the Rwandese population and of the democratization process in Rwanda;

15. *Decides* to remain actively seized of the matter.

UNITED NATIONS MEMBER COUNTRIES

Resolution 909 [Extending UNAMIR's mandate in Rwanda], 1994

Question to consider while reading: How does Resolution 909 reflect the growing doubts of some members of the Security Council about UNAMIR's role?

UN Security Council, Resolution 909 (1994), adopted by the Security Council at its 3358th meeting, on April 5, 1994, www.unhcr.org/refworld/docid/3b00f13754.html.

The Security Council,

Reaffirming its resolution 872 (1993) of 5 October 1993 establishing the United Nations Assistance Mission for Rwanda (UNAMIR),

* * *

Welcoming the valuable contribution to peace being made in Rwanda by UNAMIR,

Expressing its deep concern at the delay in the establishment of the broad-based transitional Government and the Transitional National Assembly,

* * *

Considering that the fact that the transitional institutions have not been established constitutes a major obstacle to the implementation of the Arusha Peace Agreement,

Concerned at the deterioration in security in the country, particularly in Kigali,

* * *

2. *Decides* to extend the mandate of UNAMIR until 29 July 1994, on the understanding that the Security Council will, within the next six weeks, review the situation in Rwanda, including the role played in that country by the United Nations, if the Secretary-General informs it in a report that the transitional institutions provided for under the Arusha Peace Agreement have not been established and that insufficient progress has been made for the implementation of phase II of the Secretary-General's plan contained in his report of 24 September 1993 (S/26488);

3. *Regrets* the delay in the implementation of the Arusha Peace Agreement, and urges the parties to resolve their latest differences without delay with a view to the immediate establishment of those transitional institutions still required for the continuation of the process, and particularly the implementation of phase II;

* * *

5. *Recalls* nevertheless that continued support for UNAMIR, including the provision of an additional 45 civilian police monitors as described in paragraph 38 of the Secretary-General's report, will depend upon full and prompt implementation by the parties of the Arusha Peace Agreement;

* * *

9. *Reiterates* its request to the Secretary-General to continue to monitor the size and cost of UNAMIR to seek economies;

10. *Decides* to remain actively seized of the question.

MICHAEL WALZER

From *Just and Unjust Wars: A Moral Argument with Historical Illustrations*, 1977

Michael Walzer's book-length essay on the issue of just wars was enormously influential in resetting this debate in the late 1970s. Walzer is responding to America's involvement in Vietnam and to other Cold War interventions. But he moves beyond specific responses to specific cases to develop a general study of why states (or peoples) have the right to rule themselves and what this implies about the right of other states to intervene. Reprinted here are sections of the two chapters most relevant for this game. Be sure to look at the study questions (earlier in the game book) for help on what you should be looking for as you read these sections. Only one footnote has been retained for this selection. If you're interested, please consult Walzer's book itself for citations.

Questions to consider while reading: Where do the rights of political communities come from? Why is aggression wrong in an international environment defined this way? What is the legalist paradigm? What guidelines does Walzer lay out for deciding when intervention into another state's business is appropriate? Why does he argue that intervening in another state to save its people from a domestic dictatorship (that is not committing atrocities) is wrong? What are the three possible exceptions to the general rule of nonintervention and how do they work?

CHAPTER 4: LAW AND ORDER IN INTERNATIONAL SOCIETY

* * *

The Right of Political Communities

*T*he rights in question are summed up in the lawbooks as territorial integrity and political sovereignty. The two belong to states, but they derive ultimately from the rights of individuals, and from them they take their force. The duties and rights of states are nothing more than the duties and rights of the men who compose them. That is the view of a conventional British lawyer, for whom states are neither organic wholes nor mystical unions. And it is the correct view. When states are attacked, it is their members who are challenged, not only in their lives, but also in the sum of things they value most, including the political association they have made. We recognize and explain this challenge by referring to their rights. If they were not normally entitled to choose their form of government and shape the policies that shape their lives, external coercion would not be a crime; nor could it so easily be said that they had been forced to resist in self-defense. Individual rights (to life and liberty) underlie the most important judgments that we make about war. How these rights are themselves founded I cannot try to explain here. It is enough to say that they are somehow entailed by our sense of what it means to be a human being. If they are not natural, then we have invented them, but natural or invented, they are a palpable feature of our moral world. States' rights are simply their collective form. The process of collectivization is a complex one. No doubt, some of the immediate force of individuality is lost in its course; it is best understood, nevertheless, as it has commonly been understood since the seventeenth century, in terms of social contract theory. Hence it is a moral process, which justifies some claims to territory and sovereignty and invalidates others.

The rights of states rest on the consent of their members. But this is consent of a special sort. State rights are not constituted through a series of transfers from individual men and women to the sovereign- or through a series of exchanges among individuals. What actually happens is harder to describe. Over a long period of time, shared experiences and cooperative activity of many different kinds shape a common life. "Contract" is a metaphor for a process of association and mutuality, the ongoing character of which the state claims to protect against external encroachment. The protection extends not only to the lives and liberties of individuals but also to their shared life and liberty, the independent community they have made, for which individuals are sometimes sacrificed. The moral standing of any particular state depends upon the reality of the common life it protects and the

> **TIP**
>
> Here Walzer presents a very specific notion of a "social contract." What does *he* mean by "contract?" How does his understanding differ from that of Teson?

extent to which the sacrifices required by that protection are willingly accepted and thought worthwhile. If no common life exists, or if the state doesn't defend the common life that does exist, its own defense may have no moral justification. But most states do stand guard over the community of their citizens, at least to some degree: that is why we assume the justice of their defensive wars. And given a genuine "contract," it makes sense to say that territorial integrity and political sovereignty can be defended in exactly the same way as individual life and liberty.[1]

It might also be said that a people can defend its country in the same way as men and women can defend their homes, for the country is collectively as the homes are privately owned. The right to territory might be derived, that is, from the individual right to property. But the ownership of vast reaches of land is highly problematic, I think, unless it can be tied in some plausible way to the requirements of national survival and political independence. And these two seem by themselves to generate territorial rights that have little to do with ownership in the strict sense. The case is probably the same with the smaller properties of domestic society. A man has certain rights in his home, for example, even if he does not own it, because neither his life nor his liberty is secure unless there exists some physical space within which he is safe from intrusion. Similarly again, the right of a nation or people not to be invaded derives from the common life its members have made on this piece of land—it had to be made somewhere—and not from the legal title they hold or don't hold.

* * *

The Legalist Paradigm

*I*f states actually do possess rights more or less as individuals do, then it is possible to imagine a society among them more or less like the society of individuals. The comparison of international to civil order is crucial to the theory of aggression. I have already been making it regularly. Every reference to aggression as the international equivalent of armed robbery or murder, and every comparison of home and country or of personal liberty and political independence, relies upon what is called the *domestic analogy*. Our primary perceptions and judgments of aggression are the products of analogical reasoning. When the analogy

---

1. The question of when territory and sovereignty can rightly be defended is closely connected to the question of when individual citizens have an obligation to join the defense. Both hang on issues in social contract theory. I have discussed the second question at length in my book *Obligations: Essays on Disobedience, War, and Citizenship* (Cambridge, Mass., 1970). See especially "The Obligation to Die for the State" and "Political Alienation and Military Service." But neither in that book nor in this one do I deal in any detail with the problem of national minorities—groups of people who do not fully join (or do not join at all) in the contract that constitutes the nation. The Radical mistreatment of such people may justify military intervention (see chapter 6). Short of that, however, the presence of national minorities within the borders of the nation-state does not affect the argument about aggression and self-defense.

is made explicit, as it often is among the lawyers, the world of states takes on the shape of a political society the character of which is entirely accessible through such notions as crime and punishment, self-defense, law enforcement, and so on.

These notions, I should stress, are not incompatible with the fact that international society as it exists today is a radically imperfect structure. As we experience it, that society might be likened to a defective building, founded on rights; its superstructure raised, like that of the state itself, through political conflict, cooperative activity, and commercial exchange; the whole thing shaky and unstable because it lacks the rivets of authority. It is like domestic society in that men and women live at peace within it (sometimes), determining the conditions of their own existence, negotiating and bargaining with their neighbors. It is unlike domestic society in that every conflict threatens the structure as a whole with collapse. Aggression challenges it directly and is much more dangerous than domestic crime, because there are no policemen. But that only means that the "citizens" of international society must rely on themselves and on one another. Police powers are distributed among all the members. And these members have not done enough in the exercise of their powers if they merely contain the aggression or bring it to a speedy end—as if the police should stop a murderer after he has killed only one or two people and send him on his way. The rights of the member states must be vindicated, for it is only by virtue of those rights that here is a society at all. If they cannot be upheld (at least sometimes), international society collapses into a state of war or is transformed into a universal tyranny.

From this picture, two presumptions follow. The first, which I have already pointed out, is the presumption in favor of military resistance once aggression has begun. Resistance is important so that rights can be maintained and future aggressors deterred. The theory of aggression restates the old doctrine of the just war: it explains when fighting is a crime and when it is permissible, perhaps even morally desirable. The victim of aggression fights in self-defense, but he isn't only defending himself, for aggression is a crime against society as a whole. He fights in its name and not only in his own. Other states can rightfully Join the victim's resistance; their war has the same character as his own, which is to say, they are entitled not only to repel the attack but also to punish it. All resistance is also law enforcement. Hence the second presumption: when fighting breaks out, there must always be some state against which the law can and should be enforced. Someone must be responsible, for someone decided to break the peace of the society of states. No war, as medieval theologians explained, can be just on both sides.

There are, however, wars that are just on neither side, because the idea of justice doesn't pertain to them or because the antagonists are both aggressors, fighting for territory or power where they have no right The first case I have already alluded to in discussing the voluntary combat of aristocratic warriors. It is sufficiently rare in

TIP

Walzer assumes here that, unless the rights of states are protected, the world will (often) descend into anarchy. He will therefore value the rights of states more than Teson.

human history that nothing more need be said about it here. The second case is illustrated by those wars that Marxists call "imperialist," which are not fought between conquerors and victims but between conquerors and conquerors, each side seeking dominion over the other or the two of them competing to dominate some third party. Thus Lenin's description of the struggles between have and have-not nations in early twentieth century Europe: ". . . picture to yourselves a slave owner who owned 100 slaves warring against a slave-owner who owned 200 slaves for a more 'just' distribution of slaves. Clearly, the application of the term 'defensive' war in such a case . . . would be sheer deception . . . ." But it is important to stress that we can penetrate the deception only insofar as we can ourselves distinguish justice and injustice: the theory of imperialist war presupposes the theory of aggression. If one insists that all wars on all sides are acts of conquest, or attempted conquest, or that all states at all times would conquer if they could, then the argument for justice is defeated before it begins and the moral judgments we actually make are derided as fantasies. Consider the following passage from Edmund Wilson's book on the American Civil War:

> I think that it is a serious deficiency on the part of historians . . . that they so rarely interest themselves in biological and zoological phenomena. In a recent . . . film showing life at the bottom of the sea, a primitive organism called a sea slug is seen gobbling up small organisms through a large orifice at one end of its body; confronted with another sea slug of an only slightly lesser size, it ingurgitates that, too. Now the wars fought by human beings are stimulated as a rule . . . by the same instincts as the voracity of the sea slug.

There are no doubt wars to which that image might be fit, though it is not a terribly useful image with which to approach the Civil War. Nor does it account for our ordinary experience of international society. Not all states are sea-slug states, gobbling up their neighbors. There are always groups of men and women who would live if they could in peaceful enjoyment of their rights and who have chosen political leaders who represent that desire. The deepest purpose of the state is not ingestion but defense, and the least that can be said is that many actual states serve that purpose. When their territory is attacked or their sovereignty challenged, it makes sense to look for an aggressor and not merely for a natural predator. Hence we need a theory of aggression rather than a zoological account.

The theory of aggression first takes shape under the aegis of the domestic analogy. I am going to call that primary form of the theory the *legalist paradigm*, since it consistently reflects the conventions of law and order. It does not necessarily reflect the arguments of the lawyers, though legal as well as moral debate has its starting point here. Later on, I will suggest that our judgments about the justice and injustice of particular wars are not entirely determined by the paradigm. The complex

> **TIP**
>
> Pay attention: Everything else in Walzer's text is derived from this set of assumptions

realities of international society drive us toward a revisionist perspective, and the revisions will be significant ones. But the paradigm must first be viewed in its unrevised form; it is our baseline, our model, the fundamental structure for the moral comprehension of war. We begin with the familiar world of individuals and rights, of crimes and punishments. The theory of aggression can then be summed up in six propositions.

1. *There exists an international society of independent states.* States are the members of this society, not private men and women. In the absence of a universal state, men and women are protected and their interests represented only by their own governments. Though states are founded for the sake of life and liberty, they cannot be challenged in the name of life and liberty by any other states. Hence the principle of nonintervention, which I will analyze later on. The rights of private persons can be recognized in international society, as in the UN Charter of Human Rights, but they cannot be enforced without calling into question the dominant values of that society: the survival and independence of the separate political communities.

2. *This international society has a law that establishes the rights of its members—above all, the rights of territorial integrity and political sovereignty.* Once again, these two rest ultimately on the right of men and women to build a common life and to risk their individual lives only when they freely choose to do so. But the relevant law refers only to states, and its details are fixed by the intercourse of states, through complex processes of conflict and consent. Since these processes are continuous, international society has no natural shape; nor are rights within it ever finally or exactly determined. At any given moment, however, one can distinguish the territory of one people from that of another and say something about the scope and limits of sovereignty.

3. *Any use of force or imminent threat of force by one state against the political sovereignty or territorial integrity of another constitutes aggression and is a criminal act.* As with domestic crime, the argument here focuses narrowly on actual or imminent boundary crossings: invasions and physical assaults. Otherwise, it is feared, the notion of resistance to aggression would have no determinate meaning. A state cannot be said to be forced to fight unless the necessity is both obvious and urgent.

4. *Aggression justifies two kinds of violent response: a war of self-defense by the victim and a war of law enforcement by the victim and any other member of international society.* Anyone can come to the aid of a victim, use necessary force against an aggressor, and even make whatever is the international equivalent of a "citizen's arrest." As in domestic society, the obligations of bystanders are not easy to make out, but it is the tendency of the theory to undermine the right of neutrality and to require widespread participation in the business of law enforcement. In the Korean War, this participation was authorized by the United Nations, but even in such cases the actual decision to join the fighting remains a unilateral one, best understood by analogy to the decision of a private citizen who rushes to help a man or woman attacked on the street.

5. *Nothing but aggression can justify war.* The central purpose of the theory is to limit the occasion for war. "There is a single and only just cause for commencing

a war," wrote Vitoria, "namely, a wrong received." There must actually have been a wrong and it must actually have been received (or its receipt must be, as it were, only minutes away). Nothing else warrants the use of force in international society— above all, not any difference of religion or politics. Domestic heresy and injustice are never actionable in the world of states: hence, again the principle of non-intervention.

6. *Once the aggressor state has been militarily repulsed, it can also be punished.*

* * *

Editorial note: Walzer spends the next few pages examining specific historical examples to test his arguments. He looks first at the response in 1938 to German threats against Czechoslovakia. In this crisis, the United Kingdom and France negotiated with Germany and its ally Italy to cut a deal that gave part of Czechoslovakia to Germany. They did so believing the costs of a general war would exceed the damages caused by the infringement on Czechoslovak sovereignty. Historians call this the Munich Crisis, after the city in which negotiations were held, and label the policy Britain and France adopted appeasement, because the compromise "appeased" German desires at the cost of Czechoslovak territory. Because Germany proceeded to demand more from Czechoslovakia in the months ahead, historians generally criticize the appeasement policy.

Second, Walzer looks at the case of Finland, which decided in 1939 to go to war against a vastly superior Soviet Union rather than sacrifice their principles or fellow citizens. Finland lost the war but won applause around the world for its willingness to fight rather than compromise. Thus in the Munich Crisis, the United Kingdom and France sacrificed principles to save lives while Finland made the opposite choice.

These cases allow Walzer to test the boundaries of his claims about the relationship between aggression and ethics.

CHAPTER 6: INTERVENTIONS

*T*he principle that states should never intervene in the domestic affairs of other states follows readily from the legalist paradigm and, less readily and more ambiguously, from those conceptions of life and liberty that underlie the paradigm and make it plausible. But these same conceptions seem also to require that we sometimes disregard the principle; and what might be called the rules of disregard, rather than the principle itself, have been the focus of moral interest and argument. No state can admit to fighting an aggressive war and then defend its actions. But intervention is differently understood. The word is not defined as a criminal activity, and though the practice of intervening often threatens the territorial integrity

Walzer's guiding assumption is that states deserve the right to do what they want without foreign interference. The rest of the reading will explain the exceptions to this rule. It's critical to note, however, that these are exceptions and must be justified.

and political independence of invaded states, it can sometimes be justified. It is more important to stress at the outset, however, that it always has to be justified. The burden of proof falls on any political leader who tries to shape the domestic arrangements or alter the conditions of life in a foreign country. And when the attempt is made with armed force, the burden is especially heavy—not only because of the coercion and rages that military intervention inevitably brings, but also because it is thought that the citizens of a sovereign state have a right, insofar as they are to be coerced and ravaged at all, to suffer only at one another's hands.

Self-Determination and Self-Help
The Argument of John Stuart Mill

These citizens are the members, it is presumed, of a single political community, entitled collectively to determine their own affairs. The precise nature of this right is nicely worked out by **John Stuart Mill** in a short article published in the same year as the treatise *On Liberty* (1859) and especially useful to us because the individual/community analogy was very much in Mill's mind as he wrote. We are to treat states as self-determining communities, he argues, whether or not their internal political arrangements are free, whether or not the citizens choose their government and openly debate the policies carried out in their name. For self-determination and political freedom are not equivalent terms. The first is the more inclusive idea; it describes not only a particular institutional arrangement but also the process by which a community arrives at that arrangement—or does not. A state is self-determining even if its citizens struggle and fail to establish free institutions, but it has been deprived of self-determination if such institutions are established by an intrusive neighbor. The members of a political community must seek their own freedom, just as the individual must cultivate his own virtue. They cannot be set free, as he cannot be made virtuous, by any external force. Indeed, political freedom depends upon the existence of individual virtue, and this the armies of another state are most unlikely to produce—unless, perhaps, they inspire an active resistance and set in motion a self-determining politics. Self-determination is the school in which virtue is learned (or not) and liberty is won (or not). Mill recognizes that a people who have had the "misfortune" to be ruled by a tyrannical government are peculiarly disadvantaged: they have never had a chance to develop "the virtues needful for maintaining freedom." But he insists nevertheless on the stern doctrine of self-help. "It is during an arduous struggle to become free by their own efforts that these virtues have the best chance of springing up."

Though Mill's argument can be cast in utilitarian terms, the harshness of his conclusions suggests that this is not its most appropriate form. The Millian view of self-determination seems to make utilitarian calculation unnecessary, or at least subsidiary to an

John Stuart Mill: Nineteenth-century English philosopher who wrote about what states should and shouldn't do to their citizens.

Walzer and Mill believe people have the right to self-determination—not liberty. Because political culture is extraordinarily powerful, attempts by outside forces to impose liberty on a people will inevitably fail.

understanding of communal liberty. He doesn't believe that intervention fails more often than not to serve the purpose of liberty; he believes that, given what liberty is, it *necessarily* fails. The (internal) freedom of a political community can be won only by the members of that community. The argument is similar to that implied in the well-known Marxist maxim, "The liberation of the working class can come only through the workers themselves." As that maxim, one would think, rules out any substitution of vanguard elitism for working class democracy, so Mill's argument rules out any substitution of foreign intervention for internal struggle.

Self-determination, then, is the right of a people "to become free by their own efforts" if they can, and nonintervention is the principle guaranteeing that their success will not be impeded or their failure prevented by the intrusions of an alien power. It has to be stressed that there is no right to be protected against the consequences of domestic failure, even against a bloody repression. Mill generally writes as if he believes that citizens get the government they deserve, or at least, the government for which they are "fit." And "the only test . . . of a people's having become fit for popular institutions is that they, or a sufficient portion of them to prevail in the contest, are willing to brave labor and danger for their liberation." No one can, and no one should, do it for them. Mill takes a very cool view of political conflict, and if many rebellious citizens, proud and full of hope in their own efforts, have endorsed that view, many others have not. There is no shortage of revolutionaries who have sought, pleaded for, even demanded outside help. A recent American commentator, eager to be helpful, has argued that Mill's position involves "a kind of Darwinian definition [*The Origin of Species* was also published in 1859] of self-determination as survival of the fittest within the national boundaries, even if fittest means most adept in the use of force." That last phrase is unfair, for it was precisely Mill's point that force could not prevail, unless it were reinforced from the outside, over a people ready "to brave labor and danger." For the rest, the charge is probably true, but it is difficult to see what conclusions follow from it. It is possible to intervene domestically in the "Darwinian" struggle because the intervention is continuous and sustained over time. But foreign intervention, if it is a brief affair, cannot shift the domestic balance of power in any decisive way toward the forces of freedom, while if it is prolonged or intermittently resumed, it will itself pose the greatest possible threat to the success of those forces.

The case may be different when what is at issue is not intervention at all but conquest. Military defeat and governmental collapse may so shock a social system as to open the way for a radical renovation of its political arrangements. This seems to be what happened in Germany and Japan after World War II, and these examples are so important that I will have to consider later on how it is that rights of conquest and renovation might arise. But they clearly don't arise in every case of domestic tyranny. It is not true, then, that intervention is justified whenever revolution is; for revolutionary activity is an exercise in self-determination, while foreign interference denies to a people those political capacities that only such exercise can bring.

These are the truths expressed by the legal doctrine of sovereignty, which defines the liberty of states as their independence from foreign control and coercion. In fact, of course, not every independent state is free, but the recognition of sovereignty is the only way we have of establishing an arena within which freedom can be fought for and (sometimes) won. It is this arena and the activities that go on within it that we want to protect, and we protect them, much as we protect individual integrity, by marking out boundaries that cannot be crossed, rights that cannot be violated. As with individuals, so with sovereign states: there are things that we cannot do to them, even for their own ostensible good.

And yet the ban on boundary crossing is not absolute—in part because of the arbitrary and accidental character of state boundaries, in part because of the ambiguous relation of the political community or communities within those boundaries to the government that defends them. Despite Mill's very general account of self-determination, it isn't always clear when a community is in fact self-determining, when it qualifies, so to speak, for nonintervention. No doubt there are similar problems with individual persons, but these are, I think, less severe and, in any case, they are handled within the structure of domestic law. In international society, the law provides no authoritative verdicts. Hence the ban on boundary crossings is subject to unilateral suspension, specifically with reference to three sorts of cases where it does not seem to serve the purpose for which it was established:

These are the three cases which justify intervention. Be careful to notice the qualifications Walzer introduces.

—when a particular set of boundaries clearly contains two or more political communities, one of which is already engaged in a large-scale military struggle for independence, that is, when what is at issue is secession or "national liberation";

—when the boundaries have already been crossed by the armies of a foreign power, even if the crossing has been called for by one of the parties in a civil war, that is, when what is at issue is counter-intervention; and

—when the violation of human rights within a set of boundaries is so terrible that it makes talk of community or self-determination or "arduous struggle" seem cynical and irrelevant, that is, in cases of enslavement or massacre.

* * *

The arguments that are made on behalf of intervention in each of these cases constitute the second, third and fourth revisions of the legalist paradigm. They open the way for just wars that are not fought in self-defense or against aggression in the strict sense. But they need to be worked out with great care. Given the readiness of states that invade one another, revisionism is a risky business.

Mill discusses only the first two of these cases, secession and counter-intervention, though the last was not unknown even in 1859. It is worth pointing out that he does not regard them as exceptions to the nonintervention principle, but rather as negative demonstrations of its reasons. Where these reasons don't apply, the principle loses its force. It would be more exact, from Mill's standpoint, to formulate the relevant principle in this way: *always act so as to recognize and uphold communal autonomy.* Nonintervention is most often entailed by that recognition, but not always, and then we must prove our commitment to autonomy in some other way, perhaps even by sending troops across an international frontier. But the morally exact principle is also very dangerous, and Mill's account of the argument is not at this point an account of what is actually said in everyday moral discourse. We need to establish a kind of *a priori* respect for state boundaries; they are, as I have argued before, the only boundaries communities ever have.

* * *

Editorial note: Walzer spends the remainder of this chapter examining each of these exceptions to the general rule of nonintervention. First, he analyzes cases where a people (a group that claims to make up an ethnic or national group distinct from other groups in a state) wants to secede. The historical example he discusses here, the attempt by Hungarians to secede from the Austrian empire in 1848–49, isn't relevant to the game. But the lessons he draws from this example are significant. In brief, he believes that there are occasions when intervening on behalf of such a people to assist them in achieving self-rule would be appropriate. He acknowledges, however, that while many groups claim *to be a people, few of them actually possess the unity, coherence, and longevity to support that claim. Thus it is reasonable, even necessary, for outside governments to wait and watch for a lengthy period of time to ensure that such groups are strong enough to merit assistance.*

In addition, Walzer recognizes the costs of intervention are not solely reflected in the lives and suffering of people directly involved. There may be indirect costs, and such indirect costs might be significantly higher than the costs to combatants. In particular, he recognizes that interventions may, in fact, have consequences to surrounding states. If, for instance, the intervention destabilizes the international or regional system, risking war in years to come, intervention may not be just.

Finally, he recognizes that many states intervene in such cases selfishly, interested not in helping but in what they can gain through their help. Given all of these concerns, it is best to be cautious in considering such interventions.

Walzer moves from cases in which a people wants out from under the rule of another to the broader case of civil wars in general. Here, he suggests, the principle is simple. Outsiders have no right to impose their own preferences on others. Combatants in a civil war should be left to fight it out for themselves. The only permissible intervention is that which keeps other powers out. In other words, if country A intervenes on one side of a civil war, country B may reasonably intervene to prevent country A from determining the outcome of the civil war.

The problem, then, is that civil wars often shade into something else. One side may decide that they no longer want more power within a country, but instead want to leave the country entirely. Or one side may use tactics that violate fundamental human rights or even verge on mass atrocities. In both cases, Walzer would suggest, intervention might be appropriate. But only might be. And it's hard to tell when a civil war crosses this line.

That brings us to his third exception, cases in which a state or people engage in mass atrocities. Here Walzer argues that people who engage in atrocities lose their moral right to self-determination. In his famous words, intervention is required in response to "acts which shock the moral conscience of mankind" (remember he is writing in the 1970s, when writers routinely used man instead of human). This is the section that may be most relevant to the game. However, Walzer points out, intervention often aims not at, or not solely at, relieving suffering but at seizing resources, territory, or some other kind of advantage. What, then, does that imply for governments that see atrocities happening in the world?

Humanitarian Intervention

A legitimate government is one that can fight its own internal wars. And external assistance in those wars in rightly called counter-intervention only when it balances, and does no more than balance, the prior intervention of another power, making it possible once again for the local forces to win or lose on their own. The outcome of civil wars should reflect not the relative strength of the intervening states, but the local alignment of forces. There is another sort of case, however, where we don't look for outcomes of that sort, where we don't want the local balance to prevail. If the dominant forces within a state are engaged in massive violations of human rights, the appeal to self-determination in the Millian sense of self-help is not very attractive. That appeal has to do with the freedom of the community taken as a whole; it has no force when what is at stake is the bare survival or the minimal liberty of (some substantial number of) its members. Against the enslavement or massacre of political opponents, national minorities, and religious sects, there may well be no help unless help comes from outside. And when a government turns savagely upon its own people, we must doubt the very existence of a political community to which the idea of self-determination might apply.

Examples are not hard to find; it is their plenitude that is embarrassing. The list of oppressive governments, the list of massacred peoples, is frighteningly long. Though an event like the Nazi holocaust is without precedent in human history, murder on a smaller scale is so common as to be almost ordinary. On the other hand—or perhaps for this very reason—clear examples of what is called "humanitarian intervention" are very rare. Indeed, I have not found any, but only

Walzer claims intervention is almost never only humanitarian; rather, it usually has political motives. When, then, is it okay to intervene with mixed motives?

mixed cases where the humanitarian motive is one among several. States don't send their soldiers into other states, it seems, only in order to save lives.

* * *

Editorial note: Walzer here analyzes two historical case studies of intervention in which governments acted for both humanitarian and strategic reasons. He first discusses the American decision to invade Cuba in 1898 (what Americans know as the Spanish-American War). Again the historical details aren't relevant. Important for you are the two lessons he draws. The first is that it's unrealistic to imagine that any government will ever intervene for purely humanitarian reasons. Especially in a democracy where different constituencies have different policy preferences, purity of motives is impossible. But, and this is his second point, ethical intervention requires a commitment to acknowledge and even protect the interests of the people you are intervening to support.

Walzer next analyses the case of mass atrocities in Bangladesh. From the late 1940s to the very early 1970s, Bangladesh was part of Pakistan (technically, the region was known as East Pakistan). While both East and West Pakistan were Muslim, there were linguistic and ethnic differences between the two. By the 1960s, many in East Pakistan felt very much like a minority, one discriminated against culturally and politically by West Pakistan.

Political tensions led in early 1971 to the outbreak of civil war, as the traditional military and political leaders (overwhelmingly based in West Pakistan) tried to reassert their political dominance of the country. In this fight, West Pakistani forces employed rape, ethnic cleansing, and targeted assassinations in their attempt to defeat the resistance in East Pakistan. Historians still argue about the exact numbers killed or raped, but estimates range from hundreds of thousands to a million or more.

Quickly, hundreds of thousands of refugees fled to neighboring India. The crisis promised to cost India millions in aid and threatened to destabilize northeastern India. Accordingly, India intervened in the Pakistani civil war. Critically, it did so both to stop the violence and to protect Indian interests. The intervention succeeded, and Bangladesh secured its independence in the aftermath.

Walzer concludes that we remember this as successful precisely because Indian and Bangladeshi interests coincided. Thus India's self-interest worked to secure Bangladeshi demands.

Having worked his way through these case studies, Walzer turns, at the end of the chapter, to the broader question of when humanitarian intervention is morally justified.

* * *

Governments and armies engaged in massacres are readily identified as criminal governments and armies (they are guilty, under the Nuremberg code of "crimes against humanity"). Hence humanitarian intervention comes much closer than any other kind of intervention to what we commonly regard, in domestic society, as law enforcement and police work. At the same time, however, it requires the crossing of an international frontier, and such crossings are ruled out by the legalist paradigm—unless they are authorized, I suppose, by the society of nations. In the cases I have considered, the law is unilaterally enforced; the police are self-appointed. Now, unilateralism has always prevailed in the international arena, but we worry about it more when what is involved is a response to domestic violence rather than to foreign aggression. We worry that, under the cover of humanitarianism, states will come to coerce and dominate their neighbors; once again, it is not hard to find examples. Hence many lawyers prefer to stick to the paradigm. That doesn't require them, on their view, to deny the (occasional) need for intervention. They merely deny legal recognition to that need. Humanitarian intervention "belongs in the realm not of law but of moral choice, which nations, like individuals must sometimes make. . . ." But that is only a plausible formulation if one doesn't stop with it, as lawyers are likely to do. For moral choices are not simply *made*; they are also judged, and so there must be criteria for judgment. If these are not provided by the law, or if legal provision runs out at some point, they are nevertheless contained in our common morality, which doesn't run out, and which still needs to be explicated after the lawyers have finished.

Morality, at least, is not a bar to unilateral action, so long as there is no immediate alternative available. There was none in the Bengali case. No doubt, the massacres were a matter of universal interest, but only India interested itself in them. The case was formally carried to the United Nations, but no action followed. Nor is it clear to me that action undertaken by the UN, or by a coalition of powers, would necessarily have had a moral quality superior to that of the Indian attack. What one looks for in numbers is detachment from particularist views and consensus on moral rules. And for that, there is at present no institutional appeal; one appeals to humanity as a whole. States don't lose their particularist character merely by acting together. If governments have mixed motives, so do coalitions of governments. Some goals, perhaps, are cancelled out by the political bargaining that constitutes the coalition, but others are super-added; and the resulting mix is as accidental with reference to the moral issue as are the political interests and ideologies of a single state.

Humanitarian intervention is justified when it is a response (with reasonable expectations of success) to acts "that shock the moral conscience of mankind." The old-fashioned language seems to me exactly right. It is not the conscience of political leaders that one refers to in such cases. They have other things to worry about and may well be required to repress their normal feelings of indignation and outrage. The reference is to the moral convictions of ordinary men and women, acquired in the course of their everyday activities. And given that one can make a persuasive argument in terms of those convictions, I don't think that there is any moral reason to adopt that posture of passivity that might be called waiting for the UN (waiting for the universal state, waiting for the messiah . . .) .

> Suppose . . . that a great power decided that the only way it could continue to control a satellite state was to wipe out the satellite's entire population and recolonize the area with "reliable" people. Suppose the satellite government agreed to this measure and established the necessary mass extermination apparatus . . . . Would the rest of the members of the U.N. be compelled to stand by and watch this operation merely because [the] requisite decision of U.N. organs was blocked and the operation did not involve an "armed attack" on any [member state] . . . ?

*T*he question is rhetorical. Any state capable of stopping the slaughter has a right, at least, to try to do so. The legalist paradigm indeed rules out such efforts, but that only suggests that the paradigm, unrevised, cannot account for the moral realities of military intervention.

The second, third, and fourth revisions of the paradigm have this form: states can be invaded and wars justly begun to assist secessionist movements (once they have demonstrated their representative character), to balance the prior interventions of other powers, and to rescue peoples threatened with massacre. In each of these cases we permit or, after the fact, we praise or don't condemn these violations of the formal rules of sovereignty, because they uphold the values of individual life and communal liberty of which sovereignty itself is merely an expression. The formula is, once again, permissive, but I have tried in my discussion of particular cases to indicate that the actual requirements of just interventions are constraining indeed. And the revisions must be understood to include the constraints. Since the constraints are often ignored, it is sometimes argued that it would be best to insist on an absolute rule of nonintervention (as it would be best to insist on an absolute rule of nonparticipation). But the absolute rule will also be ignored, and we will then have no standards by which to judge what happens next. In fact, we do have standards, which I have tried to map out. They reflect deep and valuable, though in their applications difficult and problematic, commitments to human rights.

FERNANDO TESON

From *Humanitarian Intervention: An Inquiry into Law and Morality*, 1988

First published in 1988, Teson's work is an exceptionally influential response to the human rights crises of the 1970s and 1980s. It is particularly important because it rejects out of hand Walzer's explanation for the origin of state sovereignty. States exist, according to Teson, to protect their citizens. When they choose to ignore this requirement or, worse, oppress their own citizens, they forfeit the protections of sovereignty.

Teson recognizes the dangers in allowing countries to intervene in the affairs of other states. But in the end, he believes the rights of individuals trump the rights of collectives or governments. Thus he is an appropriate counter to Walzer. (All footnotes have been deleted.)

Questions to consider while reading: Where do the rights of political communities come from? How does Teson compare to Walzer? Does Teson's definition make humanitarian intervention more plausible or less? What are the conditions that make humanitarian intervention admissible? What questions do countries need to ask themselves before adopting a policy of humanitarian intervention?

Fernando R. Tesón: "A Moral Framework for Humanitarian Intervention." In Humanitarian Intervention: An Inquiry into Law and Morality. *Leiden: Koninklijke Brill B.V. (2005). With permission from Brill.*

CHAPTER 6: A MORAL FRAMEWORK FOR HUMANITARIAN INTERVENTION

*T*he considerations in support of the moral justification of humanitarian intervention in appropriate cases emerge, I hope, from the foregoing critique of the noninterventionist model. In this chapter I shall summarize the ethical theory of international law defended here, in the light of which international legal materials should be interpreted. Our normative theory should be able to perform two tasks. It must try to explain in a consistent manner those norms of international law that are well settled, and it must provide guidance in difficult cases.

1. From an ethical standpoint governments are, internationally and domestically, mere agents of the people. Consequently, their international rights derive from the rights of the individuals who inhabit and constitute the state.

*I*nternational law has been traditionally articulated as a cluster of inter-state principles and norms. However, since states do not have the same moral status as individuals, discourse about rights of states must be reduced to discourse about rights held by individuals. Propositions about international rights of states can be translated into propositions about individual rights without any loss of meaning. I have suggested that, from a philosophical standpoint, only governments that are representative and respect human rights have these international rights. This is the idea conveyed by the claim that state autonomy can only be predicated of governments that conform with "appropriate principles of justice." The state's rights to political independence and territorial integrity, therefore, derive from the rights of individuals; governments do not have any independent or autonomous moral standing. This suggestion requires further elaboration.

The thesis advanced in this book ultimately rests on a fundamental philosophical assumption: that the reason for creating and maintaining states and governments is precisely to ensure the protection of the rights of the individuals. A necessary condition to justify political power exercised by human beings over their fellow human beings is that the rights of everybody be respected.

Thus states and governments do not exist primarily to ensure order, but to secure natural rights. Accordingly, my defense of humanitarian intervention presupposes some form of social contract as the proper philosophical justification of the state. States and governments exist because individuals have consented, or would ideally consent, to transfer some of their rights in order to make social cooperation possible.

I need not deal here with the issue whether the consent is actual or hypothetical. While lines are sometimes hard to draw, in most cases the oppressive nature of a regime is apparent. In an appraisal, both actual and hypothetical consent play a role: actual consent, as reflected in presence or absence of democratic institutions and effective protection of individual rights; hypothetical consent, as a philosophical standpoint from which to improve and perfect those free institutions.

Rights of governments are solely the result of a consensual transfer by the citizens of some of their rights. That "vertical contract" establishes the legitimate boundaries of political conduct. States and governments that are generally faithful to that original purpose are fully protected, in a moral sense, against foreign intervention—they hold against foreigners the rights of political independence and territorial integrity. To wage war against such states (except in self-defense) is a crime. But governments who turn against their citizens are on a different moral footing. By denying human rights they have forfeited the protection afforded them by international law. They are no longer justified *qua* governments, they no longer represent or are entitled to represent the citizens vis-à-vis the outside world, and therefore foreigners are not bound to respect them. In sum, dictators lose their international rights by virtue of the violation of the terms of the original contract—by betraying their *raison d'être*.

> Compare with Walzer. Walzer says that states, and the social contracts that establish them, evolve. Teson says they do not. Why is this important?

The theory of international law defended here—rights of states as derived from human rights—applies beyond the justification of the doctrine of humanitarian intervention. *All* international rights of states are ultimately derived from the rights of individuals. Article 51 of the United Nations Charter, which recognizes the right of self-defense against armed attack, is a forceful illustration of the humanitarian underpinnings of international law. Why is a war in self-defense morally justified? Under a human rights-based theory of international law, a war in response to aggression is justified as *governmental action to defend the rights of its subjects, that is, the rights of individuals as victims of the foreign aggression.* The use of force in self-defense, therefore, is a use of force in defense of human rights. But,

Essentially, the idea that states exist and have rights in themselves.

unless one accepts the notion (rejected in Chapter Three) of an autonomous right of the state, there is no substantial moral difference between the rights of citizens and those of foreigners, at least where basic human rights are at stake. Persons have rights as persons, not as citizens of particular states. Therefore, the same principle that justifies self-defense justifies humanitarian intervention in appropriate cases. The resistance to accept this simple conclusion springs from the continuing adherence, especially in international legal discourse, to some version of the Hegelian Myth—of the moral autonomy of the state.

*   *   *

2. A justifiable intervention must be aimed at dictators for the purpose of putting an end to human rights violations.

A military intervention must be truly humanitarian to be justified. The problem is to formulate standards to measure the humanitarian purpose of the intervention. I suggest the following reformulation of this requirement of disinterestedness. First, the intervening state must aim its military action at stopping human rights deprivations by governments. This includes overthrowing dictatorial governments where necessary. Second, collateral non-humanitarian motives (such as desire for border security and strengthening of alliances) should be such as to *not impair or reduce the first paramount human rights objective of the intervention.* Third, the *means* used must always be rights-inspired. This requirement is violated where the intervenor acts in such a way as to impair human rights along the way (for example in third nations), even if its true overall aim is to protect human rights in the target state.

Each author addresses this issue. Compare Teson's stance with the other authors.

Disinterestedness should not be measured by reference to some mythical "state will" as evidenced in statements by government officials. Rather, the authenticity of the humanitarian purpose must be ascertained by examining the *concrete actions* taken by the intervenor in the light of the human rights objective mentioned above. Some of the questions we must ask in order to assess the morality of the intervention are the following: Did troops occupy the territory longer than necessary? Has the intervenor demanded advantages or favors from the new government? Did the intervenor seek to dominate the target state in some way unrelated to humanitarian concerns? The test I suggest here avoids the difficulties of trying to determine what state officials really had in mind when they decided to intervene, whether they said that they were acting out of humanitarian concerns or for some other reason. Their actions, not their words, must count. And the final test will be whether human rights have been effectively restored as a result of the intervention.

3. Humanitarian intervention is governed by the interplay of the principles of proportionality and restoration of human rights.

*T*he principle that applies here is the well-known rule of proportionality. The seriousness of the reaction against human rights abuses must be proportionate both to the gravity of the abuses and to the probability of remedying the situation. If an oppressive government can be forced to enact democratic reforms through economic or political pressure, then those measures are preferable to forcible action and should be tried first. Military intervention, as a remedy against human rights violations, should only be resorted to when all peaceful means have failed or are likely to fail. The reason is simple: war is devastating; innocent people die, countries are ravaged and destroyed. By the same token, the intervention should be as surgical as possible: To be morally acceptable it must be narrowly aimed at the delinquent government and its military supporters, and not at the general population.

> ### TIP
>
> Pro-intervention players: Note this carefully. How can you use this in the game?

The test of proportionality, however, is not a utilitarian test. In some cases of humanitarian intervention more lives will be lost than saved. The moral imperative to fight evil sometimes overrides calculations in terms of deaths and sufferings. Proportionality must be measured in terms of the size of forcible means used compared to the evil it is designed to suppress. As shown in a previous chapter, such evil is not measured only in terms of individual utility, of human rights enjoyment, but in terms of the disrespectful nature of the dictatorial regime which is being targeted by the intervention. Under the approach suggested here, rights of innocent persons may sometimes be infringed, but only to restore human rights in a society where they are being ignored in a widespread, consistent and patent manner. In **John Rawls's** terms, "a less extensive liberty must strengthen the total system of liberty shared by all." Extending this principle to international relations,

John Rawls: English philosopher who considered what the best possible society would look like.

one might say that the hardships that result from intervening can only be justified if the intervention has strengthened the total system of liberty, i.e., human rights, shared by all, where liberty is defined in a nonutilitarian way. Yet it is important to stress that, other things being equal, humanitarian interventions that are likely to cause substantially disproportionate additional suffering should not be initiated. As indicated above, consequences in terms of suffering are important, although they should not be the only concern. There will always be need of a prudential calculation on the part of governments; indeed, this is the reason why humanitarian intervention is a right and not a duty of governments.

The principle of proportionality also dictates that human rights violations must be serious enough to justify foreign intervention. As explained in the previous chapter, human rights deprivations that justify war are disrespectful violations

Immanuel Kant: Eighteenth-century German philosopher interested in how to live a good life.

in the **Kantian** sense; that is, governmental infringements aimed at thwarting individual autonomy. This provision has two dimensions. Quantitatively, human rights deprivations must be extensive, although they need not reach genocidal proportions. Qualitatively, only the violation of basic civil and political rights warrants humanitarian intervention. As to the quantitative element, where the violation of human rights is not systematic, force should not be used. Violations of human rights may occur even in democratic societies. The test, however, is whether human rights violations are sufficiently widespread and pervasive to justify classifying that society as a repressive state. There are many well-known indicators of freedom. Is the government representative? Does it practice arbitrary detention or torture? Is there freedom of speech? Are political opponents allowed? How are they treated? Is there a minimally fair judicial system? Are people being kidnapped by government forces? It is a conjunction of these and other similar factors that turn governments into illegitimate, outlaw dictators.

While cases like Amin's Uganda and Pol Pot's Cambodia are clear instances of situations warranting humanitarian intervention, oppression need not reach those proportions to warrant foreign-supported overthrow. As shown above, all dictators guilty of disrespectful human rights deprivations are equally illegitimate, and so people have a right to revolt against them and, to that end, to seek and receive outside help. We saw that Walzer argues for the permissibility of humanitarian intervention only in cases of genocide, enslavement and mass deportation. But once he has allowed for those cases his own argument for state autonomy falls apart. Why only those cases and not others? Why should self-determination have priority over freedom from terror, torture, or suppressed speech? We are all too well acquainted with dictatorial methods to know that individuals can be denied their basic rights even if no genocide or enslavement is taking place. Governments that engage in rule by terror have no more claim to legitimacy than Amin or Pol Pot.

* * *

4. The victims of oppression must welcome the intervention.

A necessary condition for humanitarian intervention is that the victims of human rights violations welcome the foreign invasion. This requirement is met when subjects are actually willing to revolt against their tyrannical government. This definition, however, must be refined further. For there are situations where tyrants exercise extreme forms of terror that hypnotize their victims into "willing" submission. Because individuals in those extreme situations have lost their moral autonomy, the moral correctness of humanitarian intervention cannot depend on their expressed will to revolt. We must therefore qualify the requirement as follows: *Humanitarian intervention is forcible help to individuals who are willing to revolt against their tyrannical government, or who would be willing to revolt if they were fully autonomous.* It must be stressed that only extreme forms of submission of the will should trigger the applicability of this model of ideal, as opposed to actual, rationality. In most cases the victims of oppression must actually be willing to receive outside help.

This important requirement helps us put humanitarian intervention in its proper moral perspective. The aim of intervention is to rescue individuals from their own government. If the citizens whose rights are being violated do not wish to be rescued—if they consent to their government—then foreigners should not substitute their judgment for that of the citizens. Traditional critics have portrayed humanitarian intervention as unilateral action taken by foreign governments to remedy what those governments subjectively perceive as human rights deprivations. Indeed, even the word "intervention" wrongly emphasizes the standpoint of the intervenor rather than that of the victims of human rights deprivations. The definition suggested here underscores instead the essential moral link between the will of the citizens who revolt against their tyrants and the foreigners who are willing to help them. The task, then, is to determine the scope of this requirement.

Michael Walzer concedes that if "the invaders are welcomed by a clear majority of the people, then it would be odd to accuse them of any crime at all," a statement which seems to be inconsistent with his views about communal integrity. More important, the claim that only majoritarian approval legitimizes humanitarian intervention is morally weak. Such claim rules out intervention to protect minorities whose rights are being systematically denied by the government with majoritarian acquiescence. To be sure, Walzer concedes that intervention on behalf of minorities who are victims of genocide, enslavement or mass deportation is justified. But in all other cases where minorities are persecuted short of genocide Walzer's theory would deny the right of minorities to seek and receive outside help. This view is unacceptable from a natural rights perspective. There are certain limits that not even political action validated by the majoritarian process or general acquiescence may override. The requirement of local support for the intervention cannot be measured by an opinion poll among the citizens of the state.

The view suggested here instead is that the *victims themselves* must welcome the intervention. If the victims of oppression (whether or not they are a majority of the population) reject foreign intervention and prefer instead to tolerate their situation, then foreigners should exercise restraint. Conversely, if the victims of oppression welcome the intervention they are entitled to receive help, provided that the other requirements obtain, even if a majority of the population is ready to join the tyrants against the foreigners. It is worth noting that, contrary to what Walzer and others suggest, there is evidence that in recent instances of humanitarian intervention local populations have welcomed the intervenors. Similarly, in cases where the victims rejected the (benign) intervenors, as the Mexicans did during Woodrow Wilson's intervention in 1914, the results were disastrous. While the presumption should be that the oppressed people wish to be liberated from the tyrants, democratic governments must make sure as best they can before they decide to intervene that such is indeed the case.

In many situations the local support for intervention will be evidenced by a request to intervene from local leaders. In this context, it is necessary to mention here Walzer's theory of counter-intervention. Following Mill and Montague Bernard, Walzer claims that foreign intervention is justified in a civil war when it is designed to offset prior or simultaneous intervention by another foreign state. The aim of counter-intervention, he argues, is to restore the balance of forces in the indigenous struggle—to protect the integrity of the process of self-determination. Gerald Doppelt has forcefully responded to this amoral theory of counter-intervention:

> But this is a very strange doctrine. . . . [I]f one side clearly represents the democratic or liberal forces. . . and gets the external military intervention it needs and requests, would another state have the right to intervene on the side of the tyrannical government and its supporters merely to restore the original balance of Forces?

Walzer answers this question in the affirmative. So not only does he reject humanitarian intervention (except for genocide, enslavement or mass deportation) but he accepts pro-dictatorship intervention when the democratic forces are receiving outside help! I need not, at this stage in my argument, reiterate that this "neutral" rule of counter-intervention disregards the moral dimension of the internal struggle. Because in civil wars the correctness of foreign intervention cannot be disentangled from the justice of the cause, intervention in favor of tyrants is always unjustified, regardless of whether it is in response to prior intervention on behalf of the democratic, or pro-human rights, forces. Walzer's astonishing defense of foreign intervention in favor of tyrants where the democratic forces have already received, or are receiving, outside help, reveals the implausibility of Walzer's conception of self-determination as the highest value of international morality. It underscores the exalted and primary status enjoyed by the rights of states, and not of individuals, in his theoretical scheme. Put simply, noninterventionism is a doctrine that strongly supports the international status quo; it is, therefore, blind to the moral dimension of politics. Such a view cannot possibly have a place in an ethical theory of international law rooted in human rights.

GEORGE H. W. BUSH

"New World Order" Speech, 1991

George H. W. Bush became president just as the Cold War drew to a close. By nature Bush was taciturn and cautious. Yet, in his State of the Union address in January of 1992, he reflected on the end of the Cold War in almost breathless terms:

> *And we gather tonight at a dramatic and deeply promising time in our history, and in the history of man on Earth. For in the past 12 months, the world has known changes of almost Biblical proportions. And even now, months after the failed coup that doomed a failed system [an attempt by conservatives in the Soviet Union to reverse the move toward democratic capitalism by overthrowing the reforming government in Moscow], I am not sure we've absorbed the full impact, the full import of what happened. But Communism died this year.*

> *And even as President, with the most fascinating possible vantage point, there were times when I was so busy managing progress and helping to lead change that I didn't always show the joy that was in my heart. But the biggest thing that has happened in the world in my life, in our lives, is this: By the grace of God, America won the Cold War.*

The end of the Cold War allowed policy makers everywhere to imagine a different world. Often these visions were focused on domestic change. But, particularly in the United States and other great powers, they extended to reimagining the way countries should interact.

In the speech that follows, delivered not quite a year before his State of the Union address, Bush lays out his vision for the postwar world.

Questions to consider while reading: Why is this speech generally referred to as the "New World Order" speech? How does Bush imagine the postwar world will work? What role should the United States play in this world? The UN?

George H. W. Bush, Remarks at Maxwell Air Force Base War College, Montgomery, Alabama, April 13, 1991, George H. W. Bush Presidential Library and Museum, https://bush41library.tamu.edu/archives /public-papers/2869.

* * *

Here at Air University it's your business to read the lessons of the past with an eye on the far horizon. And that's why I wanted to speak to you today about the new world taking shape around us, about the prospects for a new world order now within our reach.

For more than four decades we've lived in a world divided East from West, a world locked in a conflict of arms and ideas called the Cold War. Two systems, two superpowers separated by mistrust and unremitting hostility. For more than four decades, America's energies were focused on containing the threat to the free world from the forces of communism. That war is over. East Germany has vanished from the map as a separate entity. Today in Berlin, the wall that once divided a continent, divided a world in two, has been pulverized, turned into souvenirs. And the sections that remain standing are but museum pieces. The Warsaw Pact passed into the pages of history last week, not with a bang but with a whimper—its demise reported in a story reported on page A16 of the *Washington Post*.

In the coming weeks I'll be talking in some detail about the possibility of a new world order emerging after the Cold War. And in recent weeks I've been focusing not only on the Gulf but on free trade: on the North American free trade agreement, the Uruguay round trade negotiations, and the essentiality of obtaining from the United States Congress a renewal of Fast Track authority to achieve our goals. But today I want to discuss another aspect of that order: our relations with Europe and the Soviet Union.

Twice this century, a dream born on the battlefields of Europe died after the shooting stopped—the dream of a world in which major powers worked together to ensure peace, to settle their disputes through cooperation, not confrontation. Today a transformed Europe stands closer than ever before to its free and democratic destiny. At long last, Europe is moving forward, moving toward a new world of hope.

At the same time, we and our European allies have moved beyond containment to a policy of active engagement in a world no longer driven by cold war tensions and animosities. You see, as the Cold War drew to an end we saw the possibilities of a new order in which nations worked together to promote peace and prosperity.

I'm not talking here of a blueprint that will govern the conduct of nations or some supernatural structure or institution. The new world order does not mean surrendering our national sovereignty or forfeiting our interests. It really describes a responsibility imposed by our successes. It refers to new ways of working with other nations to deter aggression and to achieve stability, to achieve prosperity and, above all, to achieve peace.

It springs from hopes for a world based on a shared commitment among nations large and small to a set of principles that undergird our relations: peaceful settlements of disputes, solidarity against aggression, reduced and controlled arsenals, and just treatment of all peoples.

This order, this ability to work together, got its first real test in the **Gulf War**. For the first time, a regional conflict—the aggression against

Gulf War: The war was waged by a U.S.-led coalition in 1990–91 in response to Iraq's invasion of Kuwait.

Kuwait—did not serve as a proxy for superpower confrontation. For the first time, the United Nations Security Council, free from the clash of cold war ideologies, functioned as its designers intended—a force for conflict resolution in collective security.

In the Gulf, nations from Europe and North America, Asia and Africa and the Arab world joined together to stop aggression, and sent a signal to would-be tyrants everywhere in the world. By joining forces to defend one small nation, we showed that we can work together against aggressors in defense of principle.

We also recognized that the Cold War's end didn't deliver us into an era of perpetual peace. As old threats recede, new threats emerge. The quest for the new world order is, in part, a challenge to keep the dangers of disorder at bay.

Today, thank God, Kuwait is free. But turmoil in that tormented region of the world continues. **Saddam**'s continued savagery has placed his regime outside the international order. We will not interfere in Iraq's civil war. Iraqi people must decide their own political future.

Saddam Hussein: President of Iraq 1979–2003.

Looking out here at you and thinking of your families, let me comment a little further. We set our objectives. These objectives, sanctioned by international law, have been achieved. I made very clear that when our objectives were obtained that our troops would be coming home. And yes, we want the suffering of those refugees to stop, and in keeping with our nation's compassion and concern, we are massively helping. But yes, I want our troops out of Iraq and back home as soon as possible.

Internal conflicts have been raging in Iraq for many years. And we're helping out, and we're going to continue to help these refugees. But I do not want one single soldier or airman shoved into a civil war in Iraq that's been going on for ages. And I'm not going to have that.

I know the coalition's historic effort destroyed Saddam's ability to undertake aggression against any neighbor. You did that job. But now the international community will further guarantee that Saddam's ability to threaten his neighbors is completely eliminated by destroying Iraq's weapons of mass destruction.

And as I just mentioned, we will continue to help the Iraqi refugees, the hundreds and thousands of victims of this man's—Saddam Hussein's—brutality. See food and shelter and safety and the opportunity to return unharmed to their homes. We will not tolerate any interference in this massive international relief effort. Iraq can return to the community of nations only when its leaders abandon the brutality and repression that is destroying their country. With Saddam in power, Iraq will remain a pariah nation, its people denied moral contacts with most of the outside world.

We must build on the successes of **Desert Storm** to give new shape and momentum to this new world order, to use force wisely and extend the hand of compassion wherever we can. Today we welcome Europe's willingness to shoulder a large share of this responsibility. This new sense of responsibility on the part of our European allies is most evident and most critical in Europe's eastern half.

Desert Storm: Code name for the military attack on Iraq.

The nations of Eastern Europe, for so long the other Europe, must take their place now alongside their neighbors to the west. Just as we've overcome Europe's political division, we must help to ease crossover from poverty into prosperity.

The United States will do its part—we always have—as we have already in reducing Poland's official debt burden to the United States by 70 percent, increasing our assistance this year to Eastern Europe by 50 percent. But the key to helping these new democracies develop is trade and investment.

The new entrepreneurs of Czechoslovakia and Poland and Hungary aren't looking to government, their own or others, to shower them with riches. They're looking for new opportunities, a new freedom for the productive genius strangled by 40 years of state control.

Yesterday, my esteemed friend, a man we all honor and salute, President Vaclav Havel of Czechoslovakia called me up. He wanted to request advice and help from the West. He faces enormous problems. You see, Czechoslovakia wants to be democratic. This man is leading them towards perfecting their fledgling democracy. Its economy is moving from a failed socialist model to a market economy. We all must help. It's not easy to convert state-owned and -operated weapons plants into market-driven plants to produce consumer goods. But these new democracies can do just exactly that with the proper advice and help from the West. It is in our interest, it is in the interest of the United States of America, that Czechoslovakia, Poland, and Hungary strengthen those fledgling democracies and strengthen their fledgling market economies.

We recognize that new roles and even new institutions are natural outgrowths of the new Europe. Whether it's the European Community or a broadened mandate for the CSCE, the U.S. supports all efforts to forge a European approach to common challenges on the Continent and in the world beyond, with the understanding that Europe's long-term security is intertwined with America's and that NATO—NATO remains the best means to assure it.

And we look to Europe to act as a force for stability outside its own borders. In a world as interdependent as ours, no industrialized nation can maintain membership in good standing in the global community without assuming its fair share of responsibility for peace and security.

But even in the face of such welcome change, Americans will remain in Europe in support of history's most successful alliance, NATO. America's commitment is the best guarantee of a secure Europe, and a secure Europe is vital to American interests and vital to world peace. This is the essential logic of the Atlantic alliance which anchors America in Europe.

This century's history shows that America's destiny and interests cannot be separate from Europe's. Through the long years of cold war and conflict, the United States stood fast for freedom in Europe. And now, as Eastern Europe is opening up to democratic ideals, true progress becomes possible.

The Soviet Union is engaged in its own dramatic transformation. The policies of confrontation abroad, like the discredited dogma of communism from which those policies sprang, lies dormant, if not mortally wounded. Much has changed.

The path of international cooperation fostered by President Gorbachev and manifested most clearly in the Persian Gulf marks a radical change in Soviet behavior. And yet, the course of change within the Soviet Union is far less clear.

Economic and political reform there is under severe challenge. Soviet citizens, facing the collapse of the old order while the new still struggles to be born, confront desperate economic conditions—their hard-won freedoms in peril. Ancient ethnic enmities, conflict between Republics and between Republics and the central Government add to these monumental challenges that they face.

America's policy toward the Soviet Union in these troubled times is, first and foremost, to continue our efforts to build the cooperative relationship that has allowed our nations and so many others to strengthen international peace and stability. At the same time, we will continue to support a reform process within the Soviet Union aimed at political and economic freedom—a process we believe must be built on peaceful dialog and negotiation. This is a policy that we will advocate steadfastly, both in our discussions with the central Soviet Government and with all elements active in Soviet political life.

Let there be no misunderstanding, the path ahead for the Soviet Union will be difficult and, at times, extraordinarily painful. History weighs heavily on all the peoples of the U.S.S.R.—liberation from 70 years of communism, from 1,000 years of autocracy. It's going to be slow. There will be setbacks. But this process of reform, this transformation from within, must proceed. If external cooperation and our progress toward true international peace is to endure, it must succeed. Only when this transformation is complete will we be able to take full measure of the opportunities presented by this new and evolving world order.

The new world order really is a tool for addressing a new world of possibilities. This order gains its mission and shape not just from shared interests but from shared ideals. And the ideals that have spawned new freedoms throughout the world have received their boldest and clearest expression in our great country, the United States. Never before has the world looked more to the American example. Never before have so many millions drawn hope from the American idea. And the reason is simple: Unlike any other nation in the world, as Americans we enjoy profound and mysterious bonds of affection and idealism. We feel our deep connections to community, to families, to our faiths.

But what defines this nation? What makes us America is not our ties to a piece of territory or bonds of blood; what makes us American is our allegiance to an idea that all people everywhere must be free. This idea is as old and enduring as this nation itself—as deeply rooted, and what we are as a promise implicit to all the world in the words of our own Declaration of Independence.

The new world facing us—and I wish I were your age—it's a wonderful world of discovery, a world devoted to unlocking the promise of freedom. It's no more structured than a dream, no more regimented than an innovator's burst of inspiration. If we trust ourselves and our values, if we retain the pioneer's enthusiasm for exploring the world beyond our shores, if we strive to engage in the world that beckons us, then and only then will America be true to all that is best in us.

May God bless our great nation, the United States of America. And thank you all for what you have done for freedom and for our fundamental values. Thank you very much.

FRANÇOIS MITTERRAND

Speech at La Baule, 1990

French president François Mitterrand, like Bush, presided over his nation's government during the end of the Cold War. But the transition from a colonial world to one of independent states was equally important to him. These two transitions intersected in 1990 in La Baule, France, at a conference of France and the African countries in the Francophone sphere of influence. At this conference, Mitterrand announced that France would offer aid "more enthusiastically" to countries that adopted a multiparty democracy (he said specifically that France would "link its effort of contribution to those efforts to move toward greater liberty"). He told conference attendees that "we must talk about democracy," adding: "You should not consider freedom to be a hidden enemy. It will be, believe me, your best friend." Mitterrand presented the following speech at that conference.

Questions to consider while reading: What is Mitterrand's vision for the relationship between France and its African friends? How has history left these countries with significant challenges? What should be France's role in helping them?

Francois Mitterrand: President Francois Mitterrand to Franco-African Summit, Address to Franco-African Summit, La Baule, France, June 20, 1990, Council for the Liberation and Change in Congo, National Security Archive Electronic Briefing Book No. 461, Edited by Arnaud Siad, Translations by Christina Graubert (Washington, D.C.: The National Security Archive, posted March 20, 2014).

* * *

*I*n any case, we are ready to help you establish this movement, which I believe to be indispensable in order to obtain the political, geographic, and economic instruments that would permit us to continue battling the crisis. But I would like to say the following: just as there is a vicious cycle between debt and under-development, there is another vicious cycle between economic crisis and political crisis. One nourishes the other.

This is why we should examine how to proceed together so that, politically, a certain number of institutions and ways of acting allow trust to be restored, sometimes trust between a people and its leaders, most often between one state and other states, in any case the trust between Africa and the developed countries. I'd like to borrow His Majesty the King of Morocco's observation, both ironic and serious, as he described the way in which democracy was established in France. It was not without evil, or repeated accidents. Expanding my talk, I will borrow the words of one of the Heads of State here this evening: the Europe we come from, we French, had, at the same time, Nazism, fascism, Francoism, Salazarism, and Stalinism, no less. . . .

Were these the models on which you have built your states, you who have taken, in the best case, just a quarter of a century? It took us two centuries to try to create order, first in our thoughts and then in reality, with successive descents; and we are teaching you about it?

We have to talk about democracy. It's a universal principal which seemed so incontrovertible to the peoples of central Europe that in the space of a few weeks, the regimes considered the strongest were overthrown. The people were in the streets, in the squares, and the ancient power, sensing its fragility, gave up all resistance, as if it had already been void of substance for a long time and it knew it. And this revolution of the peoples, the most important one we have seen since the French Revolution of 1789, will continue.

I said recently about the Soviet Union that this revolution has come from there and it will return there. The one who governs there knows it well, he who is, with courage and intelligence, leading a reform that, already, is facing every kind of opposition, that which, attached to the former system, refuse the reform, and that which wants to go faster. So the story is still unfinished. It must be said that this wind will go around the world. We already know it well: one of the poles freezes or heats up and voilà: the entire globe feels the effects. This thought does not have to remain climate-related, it applies to the society of men! . . .

Finally, we can breathe, finally we have hope, because democracy is a universal principle. But we cannot forget the differences in structures, in civilizations, in traditions, in customs. It is impossible to propose a ready-made system. It is not for France to dictate some constitutional law that would then be de facto imposed on people who have their own consciousness and their own history and who must know how to lead towards the universal principle that is democracy. And there are not thirty-six paths to democracy.

As Mr. President of Senegal reminded us, development is needed and freedoms must be learned. . . . How can you engender democracy, a principal of national representation with the participation of numerous parties, organize the exchanging of views, the resources for the press, when two-thirds of the population would be living in misery. I repeat, France does not intend to intervene in the interior affairs of friendly African nations. It has its say, it intends to pursue its work with aid, friendship, and solidarity. It does not intend to be questioned, it does not intend to abandon any African country.

This also about liberty: it is not only states that can provide it, it is citizens. Therefore, we must ask their opinion. And it is not only public powers that can act, it is also non-governmental agencies who often know the situation on the ground the best, who embrace the inherent difficulties, who know how to heal the wounds. We do not want to intervene in interior affairs. For us, this subtle form of colonialism, which consists of permanently teaching and giving advice to African states and those who lead them, is as perverse as all other forms of colonialism. To do this would be to believe that there are superior peoples, who hold the truth, and others, who would not be capable of it, but I know about the efforts of so many leaders who love their people and intend to serve them, even if not in the same way as on the banks of the Seine or the Thames. That is why we must begin a methodical study of everything to do with economic life. We must put customs arrangements in place that would prevent the tax evasion and other financial crimes that often justify the criticism we hear. Again, from this point of view, France, if you wish, is ready to offer aid in people and technology, to train officials, to be beside them. I have seen the birth of most of your states, I have known your battles to put an end to the colonial condition.

These battles often pit you against France, and only the wisdom of French and African leaders, at the end of the day, prevented the tragedy of a colonial war in Sub-Saharan Africa. It was necessary to build a state, a sovereignty, with internationally-guaranteed borders, the ones that were drawn and regulated by colonial countries, in gilded lounges of western Chancelleries, tearing apart ethnicities without understanding the nature of the terrain. And here we are: the new states have to manage the old contradictions inherited from history, they have to build a central administration, train and appoint civil servants, manage public finances, enter into the grand international circuit, often without having received the necessary training from the old colonial countries.

And we have to deal with these states, as we would with nations that have been organized for a thousand years, as is the case with France, Great Britain, Spain, or Portugal!

Customs and traditions just as deserving of respect as yours, the history and nature of these peoples, their own culture, their own way of thinking, could all this be reduced to a solved equation in a northern capital?

Really, I appeal to your reason, and I think that we know each other well enough to know that nothing will happen between us without respect or disregarding the esteem in which we hold each other. If there is dissent in some particular country, well then the leaders of the country will discuss it with their citizens. When I say democracy, when I chart a course, when I say that this is the only way to get to a state of equality when the need for greater freedom is apparent, of course I have a plan ready: representative system, free elections, multiparty politics, freedom of the press, independent judiciary, rejection of censorship: here is the plan that we have.

We have discussed this many times, and here, tonight, again in particular. I know how much some scrupulously defend their people and seek progress, including in their own institutions. Many of you said, "If you transpose the single party and arbitrarily decide on a multiparty system, some of our populations will refuse it, or else will immediately suffer from its deleterious effects."

Others said, "We have already done this and know about its disadvantages." But the disadvantages are still less important than the advantage of feeling that one is in a civically organized society.

Others said, "We have started, the system is not there yet, but we are going in this direction." I am listening to you. And, as I agreed more easily with those of you who defined a political system close to the one I am used to, I understood the reasons of those who believed that their country or their population was not ready. So who will decide? I believe that we could decide by saying that, in any case, this is the direction in which we all must go. Some have put on the seven league boots, either in civic peace or in disorder, but they have acted quickly.

Others are walking step by step. May I say that the most important thing is to go in the right direction. I am speaking to you as one citizen of the world to other citizens of the world: it is the path of freedom that you are advancing on at the same time as you advance along the path of development. Moreover, the thought can be reversed: by taking the road towards development, you are committed on the road towards democracy.

To you free people, to you sovereign states that I respect: choose your path, determine the steps and the pace. France will continue to be your friend, and if you wish, your support, internationally as well as domestically. You bring a lot to the relationship. When I see, for example, that the flow of capital that goes from the poor South towards the rich North is bigger than the flow of capital that goes from the rich North to the poor South, I say that there is something wrong.

Colonialism is not dead. This is no longer the colonialism of states, it is the colonialism of business and of parallel channels. We are speaking as sovereign states, equal in status, even if not always in means. There are all kinds of conventions between us. There are military conventions. I repeat the principle of the French policy: every time a foreign menace appears, that could attack your independence, France will be by your side. We have already demonstrated this many times, and sometimes in very difficult circumstances.

But our own role, as a foreign country, even though we are friends, is not to intervene in domestic conflicts. In these cases, France, with the country's leaders, will ensure the protection of its citizens, its nationals, but does not intend to arbitrate conflicts. This is what I have been doing as part of my responsibilities for nine years. In the same way, I will always forbid a practice that sometimes existed in the past which consisted of France trying to organize domestic political changes by plot or conspiracy. You know well that, for the last nine years, this has not happened, and this will not happen in the future.

BOUTROS BOUTROS-GHALI

An Agenda for Peace, 1992

Boutros Boutros-Ghali became the secretary-general of the UN in January 1992. He brought with him a new vision for the role of the UN in a world no longer trapped by Cold War conflict. He brought this vision forward in a report (written in response to a request from the Security Council) called "An Agenda for Peace: Preventative Diplomacy, Peacemaking and Peacekeeping," reprinted here.

Questions to consider while reading: What role should the UN play in new world as envisioned in this document? How might it go about doing that? How should the UN interact with sovereign states in carrying out this vision?

Boutros Boutros-Ghali, "An Agenda for Peace," Report of the Secretary-General on the Work of the Organization, 47th Session of the United Nations, January 31, 1992, www.un.org/en/ga/search/view _doc.asp?symbol=A/47/277.

INTRODUCTION

1. In its statement of 31 January 1992, adopted at the conclusion of the first meeting held by the Security Council at the level of Heads of State and Government, I was invited to prepare, for circulation to the Members of the United Nations by 1 July 1992, an "analysis and recommendations on ways of strengthening and making more efficient within the framework and provisions of the Charter the capacity of the United Nations for preventive diplomacy, for peacemaking and for peace-keeping.

2. The United Nations is a gathering of sovereign States and what it can do depends on the common ground that they create between them. The adversarial decades of the cold war made the original promise of the Organization impossible to fulfil. The January 1992 Summit therefore represented an unprecedented recommitment, at the highest political level, to the Purposes and Principles of the Charter.

3. In these past months a conviction has grown, among nations large and small, that an opportunity has been regained to achieve the great objectives of the Charter—a United Nations capable of maintaining international peace and security, of securing justice and human rights and of promoting, in the words of the Charter, "social progress and better standards of life in larger freedom." This opportunity must not be squandered. The Organization must never again be crippled as it was in the era that has now passed.

4. I welcome the invitation of the Security Council, early in my tenure as Secretary-General, to prepare this report. It draws upon ideas and proposals transmitted to me by Governments, regional agencies, non-governmental organizations, and institutions and individuals from many countries. I am grateful for these, even as I emphasize that the responsibility for this report is my own.

5. The sources of conflict and war are pervasive and deep. To reach them will require our utmost effort to enhance respect for human rights and fundamental freedoms, to promote sustainable economic and social development for wider prosperity, to alleviate distress and to curtail the existence and use of massively destructive weapons. The United Nations Conference on Environment and Development, the largest summit ever held, has just met at Rio de Janeiro. Next year will see the second World Conference on Human Rights. In 1994 Population and Development will be addressed. In 1995 the World Conference on Women will take place, and a World Summit for Social Development has been proposed. Throughout my term as Secretary-General I shall be addressing all these great issues. I bear them all in mind as, in the present report, I turn to the problems that the Council has specifically requested I consider: preventive diplomacy, peacemaking and peace-keeping—to which I have added a closely related concept, post-conflict peace-building.

6. The manifest desire of the membership to work together is a new source of strength in our common endeavour. Success is far from certain, however. While my report deals with ways to improve the Organization's capacity to pursue and preserve peace, it is crucial for all Member States to bear in mind that the search for improved mechanisms and techniques will be of little significance unless this new spirit of commonality is propelled by the will to take the hard decisions demanded by this time of opportunity.

7. It is therefore with a sense of moment, and with gratitude, that I present this report to the Members of the United Nations.

I. THE CHANGING CONTEXT

8. In the course of the past few years the immense ideological barrier that for decades gave rise to distrust and hostility—and the terrible tools of destruction that were their inseparable companions—has collapsed. Even as the issues between States north and south grow more acute, and call for attention at the highest levels of government, the improvement in relations between States east and west affords new possibilities, some already realized, to meet successfully threats to common security.

9. Authoritarian regimes have given way to more democratic forces and responsive Governments. The form, scope and intensity of these processes differ from Latin America to Africa to Europe to Asia, but they are sufficiently similar to indicate a global phenomenon. Parallel to these political changes, many States are seeking more open forms of economic policy, creating a worldwide sense of dynamism and movement.

10. To the hundreds of millions who gained their independence in the surge of decolonization following the creation of the United Nations, have been added millions more who have recently gained freedom. Once again new States are taking their seats in the General Assembly. Their arrival reconfirms the importance and indispensability of the sovereign State as the fundamental entity of the international community.

11. We have entered a time of global transition marked by uniquely contradictory trends. Regional and continental associations of States are evolving ways to deepen cooperation and ease some of the contentious characteristics of sovereign and nationalistic rivalries. National boundaries are blurred by advanced communications and global commerce, and by the decisions of States to yield some sovereign prerogatives to larger, common political associations. At the same time, however, fierce new assertions of nationalism and sovereignty spring up, and the cohesion of States is threatened by brutal ethnic, religious, social, cultural or linguistic strife. Social peace is challenged on the one hand by new assertions of discrimination and exclusion and, on the other, by acts of terrorism seeking to undermine evolution and change through democratic means.

12. The concept of peace is easy to grasp; that of international security is more complex, for a pattern of contradictions has arisen here as well. As major nuclear Powers have begun to negotiate arms reduction agreements, the proliferation of weapons of mass destruction threatens to increase and conventional arms continue to be amassed in many parts of the world. As racism becomes recognized for the destructive force it is and as apartheid is being dismantled, new racial tensions are rising and finding expression in violence. Technological advances are altering the nature and the expectation of life all over the globe. The revolution in communications has united the world in awareness, in aspiration and in greater solidarity against injustice. But progress also brings new risks for stability: ecological damage, disruption of family and community life, greater intrusion into the lives and rights of individuals.

13. This new dimension of insecurity must not be allowed to obscure the continuing and devastating problems of unchecked population growth, crushing debt burdens, barriers to trade, drugs and the growing disparity between rich and poor. Poverty, disease, famine, oppression and despair abound, joining to produce 17 million refugees, 20 million displaced persons and massive migrations of peoples within and beyond national borders. These are both sources and consequences of conflict that require the ceaseless attention and the highest priority in the efforts of the United Nations. A porous ozone shield could pose a greater threat to an exposed population than a hostile army. Drought and disease can decimate no less mercilessly than the weapons of war. So at this moment of renewed opportunity, the efforts of the Organization to build peace, stability and security must encompass matters beyond military threats in order to break the fetters of strife and warfare that have characterized the past. But armed conflicts today, as they

have throughout history, continue to bring fear and horror to humanity, requiring our urgent involvement to try to prevent, contain and bring them to an end.

14. Since the creation of the United Nations in 1945, over 100 major conflicts around the world have left some 20 million dead. The United Nations was rendered powerless to deal with many of these crises because of the vetoes—279 of them—cast in the Security Council, which were a vivid expression of the divisions of that period.

15. With the end of the Cold War there have been no such vetoes since 31 May 1990, and demands on the United Nations have surged. Its security arm, once disabled by circumstances it was not created or equipped to control, has emerged as a central instrument for the prevention and resolution of conflicts and for the preservation of peace. Our aims must be:

- To seek to identify at the earliest possible stage situations that could produce conflict, and to try through diplomacy to remove the sources of danger before violence results;

- Where conflict erupts, to engage in peacemaking aimed at resolving the issues that have led to conflict;

- Through peace-keeping, to work to preserve peace, however fragile, where fighting has been halted and to assist in implementing agreements achieved by the peacemakers;

- To stand ready to assist in peace-building in its differing contexts: rebuilding the institutions and infrastructures of nations torn by civil war and strife; and building bonds of peaceful mutual benefit among nations formerly at war;

- And in the largest sense, to address the deepest causes of conflict: economic despair, social injustice and political oppression.

*I*t is possible to discern an increasingly common moral perception that spans the world's nations and peoples, and which is finding expression in international laws, many owing their genesis to the work of this Organization.

16. This wider mission for the world Organization will demand the concerted attention and effort of individual States, of regional and non-governmental organizations and of all of the United Nations system, with each of the principal organs functioning in the balance and harmony that the Charter requires. The Security Council has been assigned by all Member States the primary responsibility for the maintenance of international peace and security under the Charter. In its broadest sense this responsibility must be shared by the General Assembly and by all the functional elements of the world Organization. Each has a special and indispensable role to play in an integrated approach to human security. The Secretary-General's

contribution rests on the pattern of trust and cooperation established between him and the deliberative organs of the United Nations.

17. The foundation-stone of this work is and must remain the State. Respect for its fundamental sovereignty and integrity are crucial to any common international progress. The time of absolute and exclusive sovereignty, however, has passed; its theory was never matched by reality. It is the task of leaders of States today to understand this and to find a balance between the needs of good internal governance and the requirements of an ever more interdependent world. Commerce, communications and environmental matters transcend administrative borders; but inside those borders is where individuals carry out the first order of their economic, political and social lives. The United Nations has not closed its door. Yet if every ethnic, religious or linguistic group claimed statehood, there would be no limit to fragmentation, and peace, security and economic well-being for all would become ever more difficult to achieve.

18. One requirement for solutions to these problems lies in commitment to human rights with a special sensitivity to those of minorities, whether ethnic, religious, social or linguistic. The League of Nations provided a machinery for the international protection of minorities. The General Assembly soon will have before it a declaration on the rights of minorities. That instrument, together with the increasingly effective machinery of the United Nations dealing with human rights, should enhance the situation of minorities as well as the stability of States.

19. Globalism and nationalism need not be viewed as opposing trends, doomed to spur each other on to extremes of reaction. The healthy globalization of contemporary life requires in the first instance solid identities and fundamental freedoms. The sovereignty, territorial integrity and independence of States within the established international system, and the principle of self-determination for peoples, both of great value and importance, must not be permitted to work against each other in the period ahead. Respect for democratic principles at all levels of social existence is crucial: in communities, within States and within the community of States. Our constant duty should be to maintain the integrity of each while finding a balanced design for all.

II. DEFINITIONS

20. The terms preventive diplomacy, peacemaking and peace-keeping are integrally related and as used in this report are defined as follows:

- Preventive diplomacy is action to prevent disputes from arising between parties, to prevent existing disputes from escalating into conflicts and to limit the spread of the latter when they occur.

- Peacemaking is action to bring hostile parties to agreement, essentially through such peaceful means as those foreseen in Chapter VI of the Charter of the United Nations.

- Peace-keeping is the deployment of a United Nations presence in the field, hitherto with the consent of all the parties concerned, normally involving United Nations military and/or police personnel and frequently civilians as well. Peace-keeping is a technique that expands the possibilities for both the prevention of conflict and the making of peace.

21. The present report in addition will address the critically related concept of post-conflict peace-building—action to identify and support structures which will tend to strengthen and solidify peace in order to avoid a relapse into conflict. Preventive diplomacy seeks to resolve disputes before violence breaks out; peacemaking and peace-keeping are required to halt conflicts and preserve peace once it is attained. If successful, they strengthen the opportunity for post-conflict peace-building, which can prevent the recurrence of violence among nations and peoples.

22. These four areas for action, taken together, and carried out with the backing of all Members, offer a coherent contribution towards securing peace in the spirit of the Charter. The United Nations has extensive experience not only in these fields, but in the wider realm of work for peace in which these four fields are set. Initiatives on decolonization, on the environment and sustainable development, on population, on the eradication of disease, on disarmament and on the growth of international law—these and many others have contributed immeasurably to the foundations for a peaceful world. The world has often been rent by conflict and plagued by massive human suffering and deprivation. Yet it would have been far more so without the continuing efforts of the United Nations.

* * *

V. PEACE-KEEPING

46. Peace-keeping can rightly be called the invention of the United Nations. It has brought a degree of stability to numerous areas of tension around the world.

Increasing demands

47. Thirteen peace-keeping operations were established between the years 1945 and 1987; 13 others since then. An estimated 528,000 military, police and civilian personnel had served under the flag of the United Nations until January 1992. Over 800 of them from 43 countries have died in the service of the Organization. The costs of these operations have aggregated some $8.3 billion till 1992. The unpaid arrears towards them stand at over $800 million, which represents a debt owed by the Organization to the troop-contributing countries. Peace-keeping operations approved at present are estimated to cost close to $3 billion in the current 12-month period, while patterns of payment are unacceptably slow. Against this, global defence expenditures at the end of the last decade had approached $1 trillion a year, or $2 million per minute.

48. The contrast between the costs of United Nations peace-keeping and the costs of the alternative, war—between the demands of the Organization and the means provided to meet them—would be farcical were the consequences not so damaging to global stability and to the credibility of the Organization. At a time when nations and peoples increasingly are looking to the United Nations for assistance in keeping the peace—and holding it responsible when this cannot be so—fundamental decisions must be taken to enhance the capacity of the Organization in this innovative and productive exercise of its function. * * *

49. The demands on the United Nations for peace-keeping, and peace-building, operations will in the coming years continue to challenge the capacity, the political and financial will and the creativity of the Secretariat and Member States. Like the Security Council, I welcome the increase and broadening of the tasks of peace-keeping operations.

* * *

IX. FINANCING

69. A chasm has developed between the tasks entrusted to this Organization and the financial means provided to it. The truth of the matter is that our vision cannot really extend to the prospect opening before us as long as our financing remains myopic. There are two main areas of concern: the ability of the Organization to function over the longer term; and immediate requirements to respond to a crisis.

70. To remedy the financial situation of the United Nations in all its aspects, my distinguished predecessor repeatedly drew the attention of Member States to the increasingly impossible situation that has arisen and, during the forty-sixth session of the General Assembly, made a number of proposals. * * *

* * *

72. As such ideas are debated, a stark fact remains: the financial foundations of the Organization daily grow weaker, debilitating its political will and practical capacity to undertake new and essential activities. This state of affairs must not continue. Whatever decisions are taken on financing the Organization, there is one inescapable necessity: Member States must pay their assessed contributions in full and on time. Failure to do so puts them in breach of their obligations under the Charter.

* * *

X. AN AGENDA FOR PEACE

75. The nations and peoples of the United Nations are fortunate in a way that those of the League of Nations were not. We have been given a second chance to create the world of our Charter that they were denied. With the cold war ended we have

drawn back from the brink of a confrontation that threatened the world and, too often, paralysed our Organization.

76. Even as we celebrate our restored possibilities, there is a need to ensure that the lessons of the past four decades are learned and that the errors, or variations of them, are not repeated. For there may not be a third opportunity for our planet which, now for different reasons, remains endangered.

77. The tasks ahead must engage the energy and attention of all components of the United Nations system—the General Assembly and other principal organs, the agencies and programmes. Each has, in a balanced scheme of things, a role and a responsibility.

78. Never again must the Security Council lose the collegiality that is essential to its proper functioning, an attribute that it has gained after such trial. A genuine sense of consensus deriving from shared interests must govern its work, not the threat of the veto or the power of any group of nations. And it follows that agreement among the permanent members must have the deeper support of the other members of the Council, and the membership more widely, if the Council's decisions are to be effective and endure.

79. The Summit Meeting of the Security Council of 31 January 1992 provided a unique forum for exchanging views and strengthening cooperation. I recommend that the Heads of State and Government of the members of the Council meet in alternate years, just before the general debate commences in the General Assembly. Such sessions would permit exchanges on the challenges and dangers of the moment and stimulate ideas on how the United Nations may best serve to steer change into peaceful courses. I propose in addition that the Security Council continue to meet at the Foreign Minister level, as it has effectively done in recent years, whenever the situation warrants such meetings.

80. Power brings special responsibilities, and temptations. The powerful must resist the dual but opposite calls of unilateralism and isolationism if the United Nations is to succeed. For just as unilateralism at the global or regional level can shake the confidence of others, so can isolationism, whether it results from political choice or constitutional circumstance, enfeeble the global undertaking. Peace at home and the urgency of rebuilding and strengthening our individual societies necessitates peace abroad and cooperation among nations. The endeavours of the United Nations will require the fullest engagement of all of its Members, large and small, if the present renewed opportunity is to be seized.

81. Democracy within nations requires respect for human rights and fundamental freedoms, as set forth in the Charter. It requires as well a deeper understanding and respect for the rights of minorities and respect for the needs of the more vulnerable groups of society, especially women and children. This is not only a political matter. The social stability needed for productive growth is nurtured by conditions in which people can readily express their will. For this, strong domestic institutions of participation are essential. Promoting such institutions means promoting the empowerment of the unorganized, the poor, the marginalized. To this end, the

focus of the United Nations should be on the "field," the locations where economic, social and political decisions take effect. In furtherance of this I am taking steps to rationalize and in certain cases integrate the various programmes and agencies of the United Nations within specific countries. The senior United Nations official in each country should be prepared to serve, when needed, and with the consent of the host authorities, as my Representative on matters of particular concern.

82. Democracy within the family of nations means the application of its principles within the world Organization itself. This requires the fullest consultation, participation and engagement of all States, large and small, in the work of the Organization. All organs of the United Nations must be accorded, and play, their full and proper role so that the trust of all nations and peoples will be retained and deserved. The principles of the Charter must be applied consistently, not selectively, for if the perception should be of the latter, trust will wane and with it the moral authority which is the greatest and most unique quality of that instrument. Democracy at all levels is essential to attain peace for a new era of prosperity and justice.

83. Trust also requires a sense of confidence that the world Organization will react swiftly, surely and impartially and that it will not be debilitated by political opportunism or by administrative or financial inadequacy. This presupposes a strong, efficient and independent international civil service whose integrity is beyond question and an assured financial basis that lifts the Organization, once and for all, out of its present mendicancy.

84. Just as it is vital that each of the organs of the United Nations employ its capabilities in the balanced and harmonious fashion envisioned in the Charter, peace in the largest sense cannot be accomplished by the United Nations system or by Governments alone. Non-governmental organizations, academic institutions, parliamentarians, business and professional communities, the media and the public at large must all be involved. This will strengthen the world Organization's ability to reflect the concerns and interests of its widest constituency, and those who become more involved can carry the word of United Nations initiatives and build a deeper understanding of its work.

85. Reform is a continuing process, and improvement can have no limit. Yet there is an expectation, which I wish to see fulfilled, that the present phase in the renewal of this Organization should be complete by 1995, its Fiftieth Anniversary. The pace set must therefore be increased if the United Nations is to keep ahead of the acceleration of history that characterizes this age. We must be guided not by precedents alone, however wise these may be, but by the needs of the future and by the shape and content that we wish to give it.

86. I am committed to broad dialogue between the Member States and the Secretary-General. And I am committed to fostering a full and open interplay between all institutions and elements of the Organization so that the Charter's objectives may not only be better served, but that this Organization may emerge as

greater than the sum of its parts. The United Nations was created with a great and courageous vision. Now is the time, for its nations and peoples, and the men and women who serve it, to seize the moment for the sake of the future.

AMERICAN LEADERSHIP CONFRONTING THE CHALLENGES OF A BROADER WORLD

By 1993, leaders across the Western world were concerned with Boutros Boutros-Ghali's leadership and the way he had tried to implement the ideals of his "Agenda for Peace." As discussed in Part 2 of the game book, the number of UN operations had exploded, the costs had correspondingly risen, and tangible accomplishments were few and far between.

With Republicans (especially) criticizing the UN, the Clinton administration laid out a vision for the way America would (and wouldn't) work collaboratively with the UN. The two speeches that follow, one by President Bill Clinton and the other by Madeleine Albright, the American ambassador to the UN, lay out the essential tenets of this relationship.

Questions to consider while reading Clinton and Albright: What problems do Bill Clinton and Madeleine Albright identify? How do they propose to solve these problems? What might happen if the changes Clinton and Albright envision don't occur?

BILL CLINTON

Address to the UN General Assembly, 1993

Bill Clinton, "Confronting the Challenges of a Broader World," Address to the UN General Assembly, U.S. Department of State Dispatch 4, no. 39 (September 27, 1993): article 1, http://dosfan.lib.uic.edu/ERC /briefing/dispatch/1993/html/Dispatchv4no39.html.

*M*r. Secretary General, distinguished delegates and guests: It is a great honor for me to address you and to stand in this great chamber which symbolizes so much of the 20th century—its darkest crises and its brightest aspirations.

I come before you as the first American President born after the founding of the United Nations. Like most of the people in the world today, I was not even alive during the convulsive World War that convinced humankind of the need for this organization, nor during the San Francisco Conference that led to its birth. Yet I have followed the work of the United Nations throughout my life, with admiration for its accomplishments, with sadness for its failures, and with conviction that through common effort our generation can take the bold steps needed to redeem the mission entrusted to the UN 48 years ago.

I pledge to you that my nation remains committed to helping make the UN's vision a reality. The start of this General Assembly offers us an opportunity to take stock of where we are as common shareholders in the progress of humankind and in the preservation of our planet.

It is clear that we live at a turning point in human history. Immense and promising changes seem to wash over us every day. The Cold War is over. The world is no longer divided into two armed and angry camps. Dozens of new democracies have been born.

It is a moment of miracles. We see Nelson Mandela stand side by side with President de Klerk, proclaiming a date for South Africa's first nonracial election. We see Russia's first popularly elected President, Boris Yeltsin, leading his nation on its bold democratic journey. We have seen decades of deadlock shattered in the Middle East, as the Prime Minister of Israel and the Chairman of the Palestine Liberation Organization reached past enmity and suspicion to shake each other's hands and exhilarate the entire world with the hope of peace.

We have begun to see the doomsday weapons of nuclear annihilation dismantled and destroyed. Thirty-two years ago, President Kennedy warned this chamber that humanity lived under a nuclear sword of Damocles that hung by the slenderest of threads. Now, the United States is working with Russia, Ukraine, Belarus, and others to take that sword down and to lock it away in a secure vault where we hope and pray it will remain forever.

It is a new era in this hall as well. The superpower standoff that for so long stymied the United Nations' work almost from its first day has now yielded to a new promise of practical cooperation. Yet today we must all admit that there are two powerful tendencies working from opposite directions to challenge the authority of nation states everywhere and to undermine the authority of nation states to work together.

From beyond nations, economic and technological forces all over the globe are compelling the world toward integration. These forces are fueling a welcome explosion of entrepreneurship and political liberalization. But they also threaten to destroy the insularity and independence of national economies, quickening the pace of change and making many of our people feel more insecure. At the same time, from within nations, the resurgent aspirations of ethnic and religious groups challenge governments on terms that traditional nation states cannot easily accommodate.

These twin forces lie at the heart of the challenges not only to our national governments but also to all our international institutions. They require all of us in this room to find new ways to work together more effectively in pursuit of our national interests and to think anew about whether our institutions of international cooperation are adequate to this moment.

Thus, as we marvel at this era's promise of new peace, we must also recognize that serious threats remain. Bloody ethnic, religious, and civil wars rage from Angola to the Caucasus to Kashmir. As weapons of mass destruction fall into more hands, even small conflicts can threaten to take on murderous proportions. Hunger and disease continue to take a tragic toll, especially among the world's children. The malignant neglect of our global environment threatens our children's health and their very security.

The repression of conscience continues in too many nations. And terrorism, which has taken so many innocent lives, assumed a horrifying immediacy for us here when militant fanatics bombed the World Trade Center and planned to attack even this very hall of peace. Let me assure you: Whether the fathers of those crimes or the mass murderers who bombed Pan Am Flight 103, my government is determined to see that such terrorists are brought to justice.

At this moment of panoramic change, of vast opportunities and troubling threats, we must all ask ourselves what we can do and what we should do as a community of nations. We must once again dare to dream of what might be, for our dreams may be within our reach. For that to happen, we must all be willing to honestly confront the challenges of the broader world. That has never been easy.

When this organization was founded 48 years ago, the world's nations stood devastated by war or exhausted by its expense. There was little appetite for cooperative efforts among nations. Most people simply wanted to get on with their lives. But a farsighted generation of leaders from the United States and elsewhere rallied the world. Their efforts built the institutions of postwar security and prosperity.

We are at a similar moment today. The momentum of the Cold War no longer propels us in our daily actions. And with daunting economic and political pressures upon almost every nation represented in this room, many of us are turning to focus greater attention and energy on our domestic needs and problems. And we must. But putting each of our economic houses in order cannot mean that we shut our windows to the world. The pursuit of self-renewal in many of the world's largest and most powerful economies—in Europe, in Japan, in North America—is absolutely crucial, because unless the great industrial nations can recapture their robust economic growth, the global economy will languish.

Yet the industrial nations also need growth elsewhere in order to lift their own. Indeed, prosperity in each of our nations and regions also depends upon active and responsible engagement in a host of shared concerns.

For example, a thriving and democratic Russia not only makes the world safer, it also can help to expand the world's economy. A strong GATT agreement will create millions of jobs worldwide. Peace in the Middle East, buttressed, as it should be, by the repeal of outdated UN resolutions, can help to unleash that region's great economic potential and calm a perpetual source of tension in global affairs. And the growing economic power of China, coupled with greater political openness, could bring enormous benefits to all of Asia and to the rest of the world.

We must help our publics to understand this distinction: Domestic renewal is an overdue tonic. But isolationism and protectionism are still poison. We must inspire our people to look beyond their immediate fears toward a broader horizon.

Let me start by being clear about where the United States stands. The United States occupies a unique position in world affairs today. We recognize that, and we welcome it. Yet with the Cold War over, I know many people ask whether the United States plans to retreat or remain active in the world and, if active, to what end. Many people are asking that in our own country as well. Let me answer that question as clearly and plainly as I can.

The United States intends to remain engaged and to lead. We cannot solve every problem, but we must and will serve as a fulcrum for change and a pivot point for peace.

In a new era of peril and opportunity, our overriding purpose must be to expand and strengthen the world's community of market-based democracies. During the Cold War, we sought to contain a threat to survival of free institutions. Now we seek to enlarge the circle of nations that live under those free institutions, for our dream is of a day when the opinions and energies of every person in the world will be given full expression in a world of thriving democracies that cooperate with each other and live in peace.

With this statement, I do not mean to announce some crusade to force our way of life and doing things on others or to replicate our institutions, but we now know clearly that throughout the world, from Poland to Eritrea, from Guatemala to South Korea, there is an enormous yearning among people who wish to be the masters of their own economic and political lives. Where it matters most and where we can make the greatest difference, we will patiently and firmly align ourselves with that yearning.

Today, there are still those who claim that democracy is simply not applicable to many cultures and that its recent expansion is an aberration—an accident—in history that will soon fade away. But I agree with President Roosevelt, who once said, "The democratic aspiration is no mere recent phase of human history. It is human history."

We will work to strengthen the free market democracies by revitalizing our economy here at home; by opening world trade through the GATT, the North American Free Trade Agreement, and other accords; and by updating our shared institutions, asking with you and answering the hard questions about whether they are adequate to the present challenges.

We will support the consolidation of market democracy where it is taking new root, as in the states of the former Soviet Union and all over Latin America. And we seek to foster the practices of good government that distribute the benefits of democracy and economic growth fairly to all people. We will work to reduce the threat from regimes that are hostile to democracies and to support liberalization of nondemocratic states when they are willing to live in peace with the rest of us.

As a country that has over 150 different racial, ethnic, and religious groups within our borders, our policy is and must be rooted in a profound respect for all the world's religions and cultures. But we must oppose everywhere extremism that produces terrorism and hate. And we must pursue our humanitarian goal of reducing suffering, fostering sustainable development, and improving health and living conditions, particularly for our world's children.

On efforts from export control to trade agreements to peace-keeping, we will often work in partnership with others and through multilateral institutions such as the United Nations. It is in our national interest to do so. But we must not hesitate to act unilaterally when there is a threat to our core interests or to those of our allies.

The United States believes that an expanded community of market democracies not only serves our own security interests, it also advances the goals enshrined in this body's charter and its Universal Declaration of Human Rights. For broadly based prosperity is clearly the strongest form of preventive diplomacy, and the habits of democracy are the habits of peace.

Democracy is rooted in compromise, not conquest. It rewards tolerance, not hatred. Democracies rarely wage war on one another. They make more reliable partners in trade, in diplomacy, and in the stewardship of our global environment. And democracies, with the rule of law and respect for political, religious, and cultural minorities, are more responsive to their own people and to the protection of human rights.

But as we work toward this vision, we must confront the storm clouds that may overwhelm our work and darken the march toward freedom. If we do not stem the proliferation of the world's deadliest weapons, no democracy can feel secure. If we do not strengthen the capacity to resolve conflict among and within nations, those conflicts will smother the birth of free institutions, threaten the development of entire regions, and continue to take innocent lives. If we do not nurture our people and our planet through sustainable development, we will deepen conflict and waste the very wonders that make our efforts worth doing. Let me talk more about what I believe we must do in each of these three categories: non-proliferation, conflict resolution, and sustainable development.

* * *

Editorial note: The next several paragraphs of Clinton's speech address the dangers of nuclear proliferation and of chemical and biological weapons and outline ways to limit this threat.

As we work to keep the world's most destructive weapons out of conflict, we must also strengthen the international community's ability to address those conflicts themselves. For as we all now know so painfully, the end of the Cold War did not bring us to the millennium of peace. Indeed, it simply removed the lid from many cauldrons of ethnic, religious, and territorial animosity.

The philosopher Isaiah Berlin has said that a wounded nationalism is like a bent twig forced down so severely that when released it lashes back with fury. The world today is thick with both bent and recoiling twigs of wounded communal identities.

This scourge of bitter conflict has placed high demands on United Nations peace-keeping forces. Frequently the blue helmets have worked wonders. In Namibia, El Salvador, the Golan Heights, and elsewhere, UN peace-keepers have helped to stop the fighting, restore civil authority, and enable free elections.

In Bosnia, UN peace-keepers, against the danger and frustration of that continuing tragedy, have maintained a valiant humanitarian effort. And if the parties of that conflict take the hard steps needed to make a real peace, the international community, including the United States, must be ready to help in its effective implementation.

In Somalia, the United States and the United Nations have worked together to achieve a stunning humanitarian rescue, saving literally hundreds of thousands of lives and restoring the conditions of security for almost the entire country. UN peace-keepers from over two dozen nations remain in Somalia today. And some, including brave Americans, have lost their lives to ensure that we complete our mission and to ensure that anarchy and starvation do not return just as quickly as they were abolished.

Many still criticize UN peace-keeping, but those who do should talk to the people of Cambodia, where the UN's operations have helped to turn the killing fields into fertile soil through reconciliation. Last May's elections in Cambodia marked a proud accomplishment for that war-weary nation and for the United Nations. And I am pleased to announce that the United States has recognized Cambodia's new government.

UN peace-keeping holds the promise to resolve many of this era's conflicts. The reason we have supported such missions is not, as some critics in the United States have charged, to subcontract American foreign policy but to strengthen our security, to protect our interests, and to share among nations the costs and effort of pursuing peace. Peace-keeping cannot be a substitute for our own national defense efforts, but it can strongly supplement them.

Today, there is wide recognition that the UN peace-keeping ability has not kept pace with the rising responsibilities and challenges. Just 6 years ago, about 10,000 UN peace-keepers were stationed around the world. Today, the UN has some 80,000 deployed in 17 operations on 4 continents. Yet until recently, if a peace-keeping commander called in from across the globe when it was nighttime here in New York, there was no one in the peace-keeping office even to answer the call. When lives are on the line, you cannot let the reach of the UN exceed its grasp.

As the Secretary General and others have argued, if UN peace-keeping is to be a sound security investment for our nation and for other UN members, it must adapt to new times. Together we must prepare UN peace-keeping for the 21st century. We need to begin by bringing the rigors of military and political analysis to every UN peace mission.

In recent weeks in the Security Council, our nation has begun asking harder questions about proposals for new peace-keeping missions: Is there a real threat to international peace? Does the proposed mission have clear objectives? Can an end point be identified for those who will be asked to participate? How much will the mission cost? From now on, the United Nations should address these and other hard questions for every proposed mission before we vote and before the mission begins.

The United Nations simply cannot become engaged in every one of the world's conflicts. If the American people are to say yes to UN peace-keeping, the United Nations must know when to say no. The United Nations must also have the technical means to run a modern, world-class peace-keeping operation. We support the creation of a genuine UN peace-keeping headquarters with a planning staff, with access to timely intelligence, with a logistics unit that can be deployed on a moment's notice, and with a modern operations center with global communications.

And the UN's operations must not only be adequately funded but also fairly funded. Within the next few weeks, the United States will be current in our peace-keeping bills. I have worked hard with the Congress to get this done. I believe the United States should lead the way in being timely in its payments, and I will work to continue to see that we pay our bills in full. But I am also committed to work with the United Nations to reduce our nation's assessment for these missions.

The assessment system has not been changed since 1973. And everyone in our country knows that our percentage of the world's economic pie is not as great as it was then. Therefore, I believe our rates should be reduced to reflect the rise of other nations that can now bear more of the financial burden. That will make it easier for me as President to make sure we pay in a timely and full fashion.

Changes in the UN's peace-keeping operations must be part of an even broader program of United Nations reform. I say that, again, not to criticize the United Nations but to help to improve it. As our ambassador, Madeleine Albright, has suggested, the United States has always played a twin role to the UN—first friend and first critic.

Today, corporations all around the world are finding ways to move from the Industrial Age to the Information Age, improving service, reducing bureaucracy, and cutting costs. Here in the United States, Vice President Al Gore and I have launched an effort to literally reinvent how our government operates. We see this going on in other governments around the world. Now the time has come to reinvent the way the United Nations operates as well.

I applaud the initial steps the Secretary General has taken to reduce and to reform the United Nations bureaucracy. Now we must all do even more to root out waste. Before this General Assembly is over, let us establish a strong mandate for an Office of Inspector General so that it can attain a reputation for toughness, for integrity, for effectiveness. Let us build new confidence among our people that the United Nations is changing with the needs of our times.

Ultimately, the key for reforming the United Nations, as in reforming our own government, is to remember why we are here and whom we serve. It is wise to recall that the first words of the UN Charter are not "We, the government," but, "We, the people of the United Nations." That means in every country the teachers, the workers, the farmers, the professionals, the fathers, the mothers, the children—from the most remote village in the world to the largest metropolis—they are why we gather in this great hall. It is their futures that are at risk when we act or fail to act. It is they who ultimately pay our bills.

As we dream new dreams in this age when miracles now seem possible, let us focus on the lives of those people—and especially on the children who will inherit this world. Let us work with a new urgency and imagine what kind of world we could create for them in the coming generations.

* * *

Editorial note: The next several paragraphs lay out Clinton's belief in the importance of sustainable development.

At the birth of this organization 48 years ago, another time of both victory and danger, a generation of gifted leaders from many nations stepped forward to organize the world's efforts on behalf of security and prosperity. One American leader during that period said this: "It is time we steered by the stars rather than by the light of each passing ship." His generation picked peace, human dignity, and freedom. Those are good stars; they should remain the highest in our own firmament.

Now history has granted to us a moment of even greater opportunity, when old dangers and old walls are crumbling. Future generations will judge us, every one of us, above all by what we make of this magic moment. Let us resolve that we will dream larger—that we will work harder so that they can conclude that we did not merely turn walls to rubble but, instead, laid the foundation for great things to come.

Let us ensure that the tide of freedom and democracy is not pushed back by the fierce winds of ethnic hatred. Let us ensure that the world's most dangerous weapons are safely reduced and denied to dangerous hands. Let us ensure that the world we pass to our children is healthier, safer, and more abundant than the one we inhabit today. I believe—I know—that together we can extend this moment of miracles into an age of great work and new wonders.

MADELEINE ALBRIGHT

Address to the National War College, 1993

Madeleine K. Albright, "Use of Force in a Post-Cold War World," Address to the National War College, Fort McNair, US Department of State Dispatch 4, no. 39 (September 27, 1993): article 4, http://dosfan .lib.uic.edu/ERC/briefing/dispatch/1993/html/Dispatchv4no39.html.

To me, this auditorium—this military institution—is the right place to discuss the Clinton Administration's foreign policy goals and address that most crucial of topics: the use of military force in the post–Cold War world. I believe that our national dialogue must ensure that this nation's foreign policy is clearly understood by those who might be asked to risk their lives in its behalf. And policy-makers must not only explain but listen—take the time to hear the concerns and answer the questions of our military personnel.

For almost half a century, whenever we talked foreign policy, we did so within a Cold War context. A whole new vocabulary was established of containment and deterrence, throw weights and missile gaps, subversion and domino theories. And U.S. military action was almost always related—directly or indirectly—to the Soviet threat. The world was a chessboard, and the two superpowers moved the pieces.

But then our chess rival left the table. The game has changed and the rules to the new one are still being written. Most of us do not for a minute mourn the Cold War era. But now there are those from all parts of the political spectrum for whom the new world is more confusing than gratifying. They can conceive of no threats to America that are not Cold War threats. They look at that empty chair on the other side of the chess table and counsel us to sit back, put our feet up, and lose interest in the outside world.

Obviously, America is safer and more secure than it was. Anyone who feels nostalgia for the Cold War ought to have his or her head examined. But anyone who concludes that foreign adversaries, conflicts, and disasters do not affect us misreads the past, misunderstands the present, and will miss the boat in the future.

* * *

Editorial note: The next several paragraphs of the speech address a variety of topics, ending in the question of whether America ought to focus on a unilateral or multilateral approach to its security. Albright argues it should be both.

The end of the Cold War has opened up another avenue for multilateral cooperation that had long been limited by the U.S.–Soviet rivalry—and that is UN peace-keeping. In recent years, there has been a dramatic increase in requests for UN assistance in resolving ethnic and other conflicts. The statistics by now are familiar: more peace-keeping operations in the past 5 years than in the previous 43; a sevenfold increase in troops; a tenfold increase in budget; and a dramatic but immeasurable increase in danger and complexity.

At their best, UN peace-keeping operations can be very effective. Obviously, they cannot be a substitute for fighting or winning our own wars, nor should we allow the existence of a collective peace-keeping capability to lessen our own military strength. But UN efforts have the potential to act as a "force multiplier" in promoting the interests in peace and stability that we share with other nations.

As I said earlier, territorial disputes, armed ethnic conflicts, civil wars, and the total collapse of governmental authority in some states are now among the principal threats to world peace. The UN is playing a constructive role in many such situations by mediating disputes, obtaining cease-fires, and, in some cases, achieving comprehensive peace agreements. This often requires the presence of UN peace-keepers or observers either to help arrange a peace or to help keep it.

Past UN peace missions have achieved important goals in places as diverse as the Middle East, Namibia, El Salvador, and Cambodia. To the extent that future peace-keeping missions succeed, they will lift from the shoulders of American servicemen and servicewomen and the taxpayers a great share of the burden of collective security operations around the globe.

Particularly when circumstances arise where there is a threat to international peace that affects us but does not immediately threaten our citizens or territory, it will be in our interests to proceed in partnership with the UN or other appropriate groupings to respond to the threat involved and, hopefully, eliminate it. In such cases, we will benefit not only from the burden-sharing aspects but from the ability to invoke the voice of the community of nations in behalf of a cause that we support.

At the same time, as America's representative to the UN, I know that UN capabilities have not kept pace with its responsibilities—and I have discussed this problem on many prior occasions. Those who support the goals of the UN do it no favors if they fail to speak out when its reach begins repeatedly to exceed its grasp. The UN emerged from 40 years of Cold War rivalry overweight and out of shape. Today, UN peace-keepers need reformed budget procedures, more dependable sources of military and civilian personnel, better training, better intelligence, better command and control, better equipment, and more money. These limitations are not inherent; they are correctable, and the Administration is doing its part to see that they are corrected.

We believe, for example, that the UN decision-making process on peace-keeping must be overhauled. When deciding whether or not to support a UN peace-keeping or peace-making resolution, we are insisting that certain fundamental questions be asked before, not after, new obligations are undertaken. These questions include the following:

—Is there a real threat to international peace and security—whether caused by international aggression; or by humanitarian disaster accompanied by violence; or by the sudden, unexpected, and violent interruption of an established democracy?

—Does the proposed peace-keeping mission have clear objectives, and can its scope be clearly defined?

—Is a cease-fire in place, and have the parties to the conflict agreed to a UN presence?

—Are the financial and human resources that will be needed to accomplish the mission available to be used for that purpose?

—Can an end point to UN participation be identified?

These questions illustrate the kind of consistent criteria—which do not now exist—that we are proposing that the UN take into account when contemplating new peace-keeping operations. And we are preparing guidelines for American participation that will promise greatest assistance in specialized areas such as logistics, training, intelligence, communications, and public affairs.

And although the Administration has not yet fully completed its review of our policy toward UN peace-keeping, I can assure you of one thing: This Administration believes that whether an operation is multilateral or unilateral, whether the troops are U.S. or foreign, young men and women should not be sent in harm's way without a clear mission, competent commanders, sensible rules of engagement, and the means required to get the job done. The credibility of UN peace operations should hinge not on how many missions there are but on the quality of planning, the degree of professionalism demonstrated, and the extent to which mission objectives are achieved.

America under President Clinton will be a strong supporter of the UN. We take seriously President Truman's pledge to the first UN General Assembly that America will work to help the UN "not as a temporary expedient but as a permanent partnership."

At the same time, we understand that there are limits to what that partnership can achieve for the United States. Adlai Stevenson used to refer to the UN as the "meeting house of the family of man," which it is, but it is a very large family. It is the ultimate committee. It reflects the broadest possible diversity of viewpoints. As Americans, we command enormous influence there because of our power and the power of our ideals. But we cannot rely on the UN as a substitute guarantor for the vital interests of the United States. The Berlin Wall would be upright today if we had relied on the UN to contain communism. That ceremony on the front lawn of the White House 2 weeks ago would never have taken place if America had subcontracted to others the job of helping Israel to survive.

Sending American military forces into dangerous situations is the most difficult decision any President can make. History teaches us that public support for such decisions is essential and that in each such circumstance Americans are entitled to the facts.

The Administration has welcomed and takes very seriously the Senate's recent request to review our policy in Somalia. We have also begun, and will continue, a regular series of close consultations with the Congress and a dialogue with the public on our policy toward Bosnia.

I have spoken at length in public speeches and congressional testimony about both issues, and both are about to enter a new phase. Bosnia may be witness to a negotiated peace that will present the international community with its most daunting peace-keeping task ever. Yesterday, the Security Council approved a resolution setting out clearly that the UN's principal goal in Somalia is to bring about the political reconciliation of that long-suffering country, in part through the establishment of basic civic institutions, such as a functioning judiciary and police. In the weeks ahead, we will continue our consultations on Somalia, Bosnia, and the full range of national security and peace-keeping issues.

Now, let me summarize my message here today. The world has changed, and the Cold War national security framework is now obsolete. The Clinton Administration is fashioning a new framework that is more diverse and flexible than the old—a framework that will advance American interests, promote American values, and preserve American leadership. We will choose the means to implement this framework on a case-by-case basis, relying on diplomacy whenever possible, on force when absolutely necessary. If American servicemen and servicewomen are sent into combat, they will go with the training, the equipment, the support, and the leadership they need to get the job done.

Recognizing that global solutions are required to global problems, the tools that America will use to carry out its foreign policy will be both unilateral and multilateral. Other nations and institutions can and should be asked to bear a substantial part of the burden of advancing common interests. We have strong reason to help build a United Nations that is increasingly able and effective. But America will never entrust its destiny to other than American hands.

Finally, in keeping with a bipartisan tradition that stretches back a half-century, America will remain engaged in the world. It was fifty years ago this month that the Republican congressional leadership, mindful of what America's periodic tendency toward isolationism had done to the League of Nations, first went on record in support of an international organization "to prevent military aggression and attain permanent peace." Senator Arthur Vandenberg sponsored that resolution, in his words:

> To end the miserable notion . . . that the Republican Party will return to its foxhole when the last shot in this war has been fired and will blindly let the world rot in its own anarchy.

Under the Clinton Administration, our nation will not retreat into a post–Cold War foxhole. Under the President's leadership, we will be called upon to work together, Republican and Democrat, civilian and military, public official and private citizen, to protect America and build a better world.

AMERICAN RESPONSES TO MOGADISHU

The loss of American lives during the battle of Mogadishu dramatically escalated the political arguments over the American relationship with the UN. The following two speeches illustrate this. The first, by Jesse Helms, the long-serving senator from North Carolina, gives an example of Republican attacks on President Clinton for handing over American sovereignty to the UN. At least a dozen other senators and congressmen, most but not all Republicans, made similar speeches that day or the day after. The second, by Clinton himself, tries to triangulate between demands for the United States to abandon the UN and contrasting calls to honor the UN's mission and vision in the world.

Questions to consider while reading Helms and Clinton: In what ways does Jesse Helms criticize Bill Clinton's foreign policy? Why does he include the UN in this criticism? What outcome would Helms like to see? How does Clinton defend his own actions? What policy does he want the United States to pursue after Mogadishu? How does Clinton present the relationship between the United States and the UN?

JESSE HELMS

Address To Congress, 1993

Jesse Helms, Address to Congress, October 6, 1993, Congressional Record—Senate, *pp. 23798–99.*

Mr. President, nearly 11 months have passed since U.S. military personnel landed in Somalia for the clearly stated purpose of alleviating suffering among so many of the pitiful people of that country. Constant and repeated scenes of starving Somalian people tugged at the hearts of most of us, and the United States properly proceeded to deliver humanitarian aid to them.

That was the origin of our involvement in Somalia. I had no objection to that. As a matter of fact, I approved of it, and said so at the time, just so long as we limited our involvement to humanitarian purposes. I said that over and over again on this floor and elsewhere, which does not make a prophet out of me, but I have some feeling of comfort that at least I understood what the potential could be in the wrong hands.

How things have changed, Mr. President, for the worst. On television this week, the American people have seen the bodies of two U.S. soldiers dragged through the streets of Mogadishu by a screaming, cheering crowd of Somali men and women.

They have seen video footage of a young American soldier, hurt and bleeding, taken hostage and held against his will.

A week ago, following the shooting down of a U.S. helicopter, there was the horrifying footage of Somalis brandishing pieces of burned flesh which they triumphantly boasted were the remains of an American serviceman.

The question, Mr. President, is: Are these the people our Government sent our young men and women to Somalia to save from starvation just 11 months ago? To call this a mission of "humanitarian intervention" is a tragic mischaracterization.

On December 4 of last year, President Bush emphasized to the Members of this Senate that the intervention in Somalia would be limited, assuring, and I quote the President, Mr. Bush, "Our mission has a limited objective, to open the supply routes, to get the food moving, and to prepare the way for a U.N. peacekeeping force to keep it moving. This operation is not open ended."

Well, look at it today.

Mr. President, on May 4 of this year, the United States officially turned over the operation to the United Nations, and that brings up another question that a lot of us in the Senate had questions about or doubts about. That was the placing of American servicemen under the command of foreign commanders. I never envisioned, and certainly I never approved, letting anybody with the United Nations be in charge of the lives of American servicemen. I do not think many Americans would have agreed to that in any event.

But instead of keeping the food moving as we were promised by President Bush—and he made that promise in good faith—the United Nations, led by Secretary General Boutros-Ghali, set as its objective something called nation building. Mr. President, I submit that building a nation is indeed an open-ended commitment, and that is not what we were told last December when we made the decision. So everything logical has been turned on its head, and now we have dead boys coming home in body bags.

But wait. There is more. The objectives continue to change. On Monday, after the American people learned that at least—at least—12 American soldiers had been killed and five U.S. helicopters had been shot down in a single battle, Secretary of State Warren Christopher said that the United States would not leave Somalia until a "secure environment" had been established. By whose authority did he make that statement?

Forgive me, Mr. President, but has the U.S. Constitution been rewritten while nobody was looking? Does the Secretary of State, or for that matter, President Clinton or any other President, now presume to have the authority to declare war? That is what we are talking about.

Mr. President, the families of our soldiers must not be forced to wait until a secure environment is established. They must not be forced to wait until husbands and brothers and fathers appear on the television screens as hostages or casualties dragged through the streets of a far-off land.

A few months ago, as I recall, after 23 Pakistani soldiers were ambushed and killed in Somalia, the distinguished Congressman Ben Gilman and I joined in writing a letter to Secretary Christopher inquiring whether, in Secretary Christopher's opinion, the United States was involved in hostilities in Somalia. We received a response from Mr. Christopher assuring us that the United States was not engaged in hostilities and was not involved in "sustained military action." Maybe so. But I wonder, Mr. President, how many more American servicemen will come home in body bags before we are engaged in "hostilities." By the way, how does the State Department define the word "sustained"?

All of which means that I support the able Senator from West Virginia—who, by the way, was born in North Carolina—Senator Robert C. Byrd, and others in efforts to bring an end to this tragic situation. The United States did its best to deliver aid and assistance to the victims of chaos in Somalia as promised by George Bush last December. But now we find ourselves involved there in a brutal war, in an urban environment, with the hands of our young soldiers tied behind their backs, under the command of a cumbersome United Nations bureaucracy, and fighting Somalia because we tried to extend helping hands to the starving people of that far-off land.

Mr. President, the United States has no constitutional authority, as I see it, to sacrifice U.S. soldiers to Boutros-Ghali's vision of multilateral peacemaking. Again, I share the view of Senator Byrd that the time to get out is now. We can take care of that criminal warlord over there. We have the means to do it and the capacity to do it. But it ought to be done by the United Nations.

I do not want to play in any more U.N. games. I do not want any more of our people under the thumb of any U.N. commander—none.

As a matter of fact, while we are at it, it is high time we reviewed the War Powers Act, which, in the judgment of this Senator, should never have been passed in the first place. The sole constitutional authority to declare war rests, according to our Founding Fathers, right here in the Congress of the United States, and not on Pennsylvania Avenue. I voted against the War Powers Act. If it were to come up again today, I would vote against it. I have never regretted my opposition to it.

BILL CLINTON

Address to the Nation, 1993

Bill Clinton, "Address to the Nation on Somalia," October 7, 1993, John T. Woolley, The American Presidency Project, www.presidency.ucsb.edu/ws/index.php?pid=47180&st=&st1.

*T*oday I want to talk with you about our Nation's military involvement in Somalia. A year ago, we all watched with horror as Somali children and their families lay dying by the tens of thousands, dying the slow, agonizing death of starvation, a starvation brought on not only by drought, but also by the anarchy that then prevailed in that country.

This past weekend we all reacted with anger and horror as an armed Somali gang desecrated the bodies of our American soldiers and displayed a captured American pilot, all of them soldiers who were taking part in an international effort to end the starvation of the Somali people themselves. These tragic events raise hard questions about our effort in Somalia. Why are we still there? What are we trying to accomplish? How did a humanitarian mission turn violent? And when will our people come home?

These questions deserve straight answers. Let's start by remembering why our troops went into Somalia in the first place. We went because only the United States could help stop one of the great human tragedies of this time. A third of a million people had died of starvation and disease. Twice that many more were at risk of dying. Meanwhile, tons of relief supplies piled up in the capital of Mogadishu because a small number of Somalis stopped food from reaching their own countrymen.

Our consciences said, enough. In our Nation's best tradition, we took action with bipartisan support. President Bush sent in 28,000 American troops as part of a United Nations humanitarian mission. Our troops created a secure environment so that food and medicine could get through. We saved close to one million lives. And throughout most of Somalia, everywhere but in Mogadishu, life began returning to normal. Crops are growing. Markets are reopening. So are schools and hospitals. Nearly a million Somalis still depend completely on relief supplies, but at least the starvation is gone. And none of this would have happened without American leadership and America's troops.

Until June, things went well, with little violence. The United States reduced our troop presence from 28,000 down to less than 5,000, with other nations picking up where we left off. But then in June, the people who caused much of the problem in the beginning started attacking American, Pakistani, and other troops who were there just to keep the peace.

Rather than participate in building the peace with others, these people sought to fight and to disrupt, even if it means returning Somalia to anarchy and mass famine. And make no mistake about it, if we were to leave Somalia tomorrow, other nations would leave, too. Chaos would resume. The relief effort would stop, and starvation soon would return.

That knowledge has led us to continue our mission. It is not our job to rebuild Somalia's society or even to create a political process that can allow Somalia's clans to live and work in peace. The Somalis must do that for themselves. The United Nations and many African states are more than willing to help. But we, we in the United States must decide whether we will give them enough time to have a reasonable chance to succeed.

We started this mission for the right reasons, and we're going to finish it in the right way. In a sense, we came to Somalia to rescue innocent people in a burning house. We've nearly put the fire out, but some smoldering embers remain. If we leave them now, those embers will reignite into flames, and people will die again. If we stay a short while longer and do the right things, we've got a reasonable chance of cooling off the embers and getting other firefighters to take our place.

We also have to recognize that we cannot leave now and still have all our troops present and accounted for. And I want you to know that I am determined to work for the security of those Americans missing or held captive. Anyone holding an American right now should understand, above all else, that we will hold them strictly responsible for our soldiers' well-being. We expected them to be well-treated, and we expect them to be released.

So now we face a choice. Do we leave when the job gets tough, or when the job is well done? Do we invite a return of mass suffering, or do we leave in a way that gives the Somalis a decent chance to survive?

Recently, General Colin Powell said this about our choices in Somalia: "Because things get difficult, you don't cut and run. You work the problem and try to find a correct solution." I want to bring our troops home from Somalia. Before the events of this week, as I said, we had already reduced the number of our troops there from 28,000 to less than 5,000. We must complete that withdrawal soon, and I will. But we must also leave on our terms. We must do it right. And here is what I intend to do.

This past week's events make it clear that even as we prepare to withdraw from Somalia, we need more strength there. We need more armor, more air power, to ensure that our people are safe and that we can do our job. Today I have ordered 1,700 additional Army troops and 104 additional armored vehicles to Somalia to protect our troops and to complete our mission. I've also ordered an aircraft carrier and two amphibious groups with 3,600 combat Marines to be stationed offshore. These forces will be under American command.

Their mission, what I am asking these young Americans to do, is the following:

First, they are there to protect our troops and our bases. We did not go to Somalia with a military purpose. We never wanted to kill anyone. But those who attack our soldiers must know they will pay a very heavy price.

Second, they are there to keep open and secure the roads, the port, and the lines of communication that are essential for the United Nations and the relief workers to keep the flow of food and supplies and people moving freely throughout the country so that starvation and anarchy do not return.

Third, they are there to keep the pressure on those who cut off relief supplies and attacked our people, not to personalize the conflict but to prevent a return to anarchy.

Fourth, through their pressure and their presence, our troops will help to make it possible for the Somali people, working with others, to reach agreements among themselves so that they can solve their problems and survive when we leave. That is our mission.

I am proposing this plan because it will let us finish leaving Somalia on our own terms and without destroying all that two administrations have accomplished there. For, if we were to leave today, we know what would happen. Within months, Somali children again would be dying in the streets. Our own credibility with friends and allies would be severely damaged. Our leadership in world affairs would be undermined at the very time when people are looking to America to help promote peace and freedom in the post–Cold War world. And all around the world, aggressors, thugs, and terrorists will conclude that the best way to get us to change our policies is to kill our people. It would be open season on Americans.

That is why I am committed to getting this job done in Somalia, not only quickly but also effectively. To do that, I am taking steps to ensure troops from other nations are ready to take the place of our own soldiers. We've already withdrawn some 20,000 troops, and more than that number have replaced them from over two dozen other nations. Now we will intensify efforts to have other countries deploy more troops to Somalia to assure that security will remain when we're gone.

We'll complete the replacement of U.S. military logistics personnel with civilian contractors who can provide the same support to the United Nations. While we're taking military steps to protect our own people and to help the U.N. maintain a secure environment, we must pursue new diplomatic efforts to help the Somalis find a political solution to their problems. That is the only kind of outcome that can endure.

For fundamentally, the solution to Somalia's problems is not a military one, it is political. Leaders of the neighboring African states, such as Ethiopia and Eritrea, have offered to take the lead in efforts to build a settlement among the Somali people that can preserve order and security. I have directed my representatives to pursue such efforts vigorously. And I've asked Ambassador Bob Oakley, who served effectively in two administrations as our representative in Somalia, to travel again to the region immediately to advance this process.

Obviously, even then there is no guarantee that Somalia will rid itself of violence and suffering. But at least we will have given Somalia a reasonable chance. This week some 15,000 Somalis took to the streets to express sympathy for our losses, to thank us for our effort. Most Somalis are not hostile to us but grateful. And they want to use this opportunity to rebuild their country.

It is my judgment and that of my military advisers that we may need up to 6 months to complete these steps and to conduct an orderly withdrawal. We'll do what we can to complete the mission before then. All American troops will be out of Somalia no later than March the 31st, except for a few hundred support personnel in noncombat roles.

If we take these steps, if we take the time to do the job right, I am convinced we will have lived up to the responsibilities of American leadership in the world. And we will have proved that we are committed to addressing the new problems of a new era.

When our troops in Somalia came under fire this last weekend, we witnessed a dramatic example of the heroic ethic of our American military. When the first Black Hawk helicopter was downed this weekend, the other American troops didn't retreat although they could have. Some 90 of them formed a perimeter around the helicopter, and they held that ground under intensely heavy fire. They stayed with their comrades. That's the kind of soldiers they are. That's the kind of people we are.

So let us finish the work we set out to do. Let us demonstrate to the world, as generations of Americans have done before us, that when Americans take on a challenge, they do the job right.

Let me express my thanks and my gratitude and my profound sympathy to the families of the young Americans who were killed in Somalia. My message to you is, your country is grateful, and so is the rest of the world, and so are the vast majority of the Somali people. Our mission from this day forward is to increase our strength, do our job, bring our soldiers out, and bring them home.

Thank you, and God bless America.

APPENDIX A

BOB'S RULES OF ORDER, OR HOW UNSC MEETINGS WORK IN *THE NEEDS OF OTHERS*

Many organizations use a standard set of rules for running meetings. This procedure is known as Robert's Rules of Order and is intended to ensure meetings run smoothly, fairly, and peacefully.

These rules are long and complex and are often misused. While I hope the game will teach you a little bit about how to run an effective meeting, that's not its central purpose.

Instead, *The Needs of Others* will use a radically simplified set of rules, based on Robert's Rules. They are meant to make the game easier to play and allow you to focus on the intellectual debates and the decisions you need to make.

Recognize that any set of rules privileges some and disadvantages others. You may find some players are unwilling to play by these rules. This game book discusses some ways this might happen. You'll discover others on your own. The GM is the final arbiter of any dispute over the rules. The GM, however, will often remain silent and force you to solve the problem on your own.

1. The chair of the Security Council runs Security Council meetings. It is this player's responsibility to create and publicize an agenda; to begin and end the meetings; to make sure all members of the UNSC can follow discussions; and to manage proposals, discussions, and votes.

   a. Agendas in Bob's Rules are informal and advisory rather than formal. In other words—the chair must allow players to make a proposal not on the agenda. However, the chair may choose to put it at the end of the scheduled agenda. If the chair wants to change the agenda in the middle, that's fine.

   b. The chair may allow (or not) players who do not belong to the UNSC to make statements and/or ask questions. A member of the UNSC may propose the council allow (or prohibit) one or more non-UNSC player(s) to participate. If so, the UNSC must vote on this proposal and follow the result.

2. Members of the UNSC should tell the chair if they wish to make formal (prepared before class) speeches. They should do so before the class begins—ideally twenty-four hours before. Ordinarily, the chair will allow members of the UNSC to ask follow-up questions. *In consultation with you*, the chair may limit the length of this question-and-answer period.

3. Ordinarily, members of the UNSC will demonstrate their desire to talk by raising their hands or walking to the podium.

   a. A player at the podium automatically gets precedence over all other speakers.

   b. The chair may choose to allow people to speak without raising their hands. The chair should ensure players raising their hands are allowed to speak in a timely way. The chair may decide *not* to allow anyone to talk without first raising a hand.

4. Proposals

   a. A player wishing to make a formal proposal should do so by saying "I move that . . ." (*not* "I motion that").

   b. Once someone has made a proposal, the chair should ask if there is a second to the proposal. If you would like to discuss or support the proposal, indicate this by saying "I second." If no one is willing to second a proposal, it is automatically withdrawn. This way, you don't waste time discussing proposals that will never pass.

   c. Once someone has seconded the proposal, the members of the UNSC may discuss the proposal—ask questions, seek clarification, make objections, indicate opposition, and so on.

   d. A player may propose a change (amendment) to the motion. To do so, the player will say, "I move to amend the proposal . . ." and state the proposed change. If the person who first made the motion agrees, the motion is amended and discussion will continue on the revised proposal. If the person who first made the motion rejects the amendment, the person proposing the amendment may ask the UNSC to vote to amend the motion anyway. The usual rules apply to this vote—60 percent must vote yes and a P5 member may veto.

   e. The chair of the UNSC *does* get to vote.

   f. When all players have had a chance to ask questions or make their case, the chair will hold a vote. The chair may decide when enough discussion has happened. The chair must allow players a chance to participate but may choose to move to a vote when players are obviously stalling. The GM has the final word if the chair seems to violate these principles.

APPENDIX B: LIST OF COMMON ABBREVIATIONS

BBTG	broad-based transitional government
DPKO	Department of Peacekeeping Operations
EU	European Union
FCO	Foreign and Commonwealth Office (United Kingdom)
HRW	Human Rights Watch
ICRC	International Committee of the Red Cross
MSF	Médicins sans Frontieres (i.e., Doctors without Borders)
NSC	National Security Council (United States)
NGO	nongovernmental organization (think tanks, nonprofit charitable organizations, and such)
OAU	Organization of African Unity
P5	the five permanent nations on the UNSC
PDD5	Presidential Decision Directive 5
RPF	Rwandan Patriotic Front (the armed forces that invaded Rwanda in 1990)
RTLM	Radio-Télévision Libre des Mille Collines (Rwandan radio station broadcasting extremist anti-Tutsi propaganda)
UNAMIR	United Nations Assistance Mission for Rwanda
UNSC	United Nations Security Council

SELECTED BIBLIOGRAPHY

BACKGROUND TEXTS ON THE HISTORY OF RWANDA

Des Forges, Alison. *Defeat Is the Only Bad News: Rwanda Under Musinga, 1896–1931*. Madison: University of Wisconsin Press, 2011.

Desrosiers, Marie-Eve and Susan Thomson. "Rhetorical Legacies of Leadership: Projections of 'Benevolent Leadership' in Pre- and Post-Genocide Rwanda." *Journal of Modern African Studies* 49, no. 3 (2011): 429–53.

Newbury, Catharine. *The Cohesion of Oppression: Client-ship and Ethnicity in Rwanda, 1860–1960*. New York: Columbia University Press, 1988.

Reed, W. C. "Exile, Reform and the Rise of the Rwandan Patriotic Front." *Journal of Modern African Studies* 34 (1996): 479–501.

Uvin, Peter. *Aiding Violence: The Development Enterprise in Rwanda*. West Hartford, CT: Kumarian Press, 1998.

Vansina, Jan. *Antecedents to Modern Rwanda: The Nyiginya Kingdom*. Madison: University of Wisconsin Press, 2004.

BACKGROUND TEXTS ON GENOCIDE IN RWANDA

Dallaire, Roméo. *Shake Hands with the Devil: The Failure of Humanity in Rwanda*. New York: Carroll & Graf, 2004.

Des Forges, Alison. *Leave None to Tell the Story: Genocide in Rwanda*. New York: Human Rights Watch, 1999.

Gourevitch, Philip. *We Wish to Inform You That Tomorrow We Will Be Killed with Our Families: Stories from Rwanda*. New York: Farrar, Straus & Giroux, 1998.

Guichaoua, Andre. *From War to Genocide: Criminal Politics in Rwanda, 1990–1994*. Madison: University of Wisconsin Press, 2015.

Kuperman, Alan. "Provoking Genocide: A Revised History of the Rwanda Patriotic Front." *Journal of Genocide Research* 6 (2004): 61–84.

Kuperman, Alan. *The Limits of Humanitarian Intervention: Genocide in Rwanda*. Washington, DC: Brookings Institution Press, 2001.

Melvern, Linda. *A People Betrayed: The Role of the West in Rwanda's Genocide*. London: Zed Books, 2000.

Melvern, Linda. *Conspiracy to Murder: The Rwanda Genocide and the International Community*. London: Verso, 2004.

Newbury, Catharine. "Ethnicity and the Politics of History in Rwanda." *Africa Today* 45, no. 1 (1998): 7–24.

Newbury, Catharine and David Newbury. "A Catholic Mass in Kigali: Contested Views of the Genocide and Ethnicity in Rwanda." *Canadian Journal of African Studies / Revue Canadienne des Études Africaines* 33, no. 2/3 (1999): 292–328. [Special Issue: French-Speaking Central Africa: Political Dynamics of Identities and Representations.]

Prunier, Gérard. *The Rwanda Crisis: History of a Genocide*. New York: Columbia University Press, 1997.

Straus, Scott. *Making and Unmaking Nations: War, Leadership, and Genocide in Modern Africa*. Ithaca, NY: Cornell University Press, 2015.

Straus, Scott. *The Order of Genocide: Race, Power, and War in Rwanda*. Ithaca, NY: Cornell University Press, 2006.

BACKGROUND TEXTS ON ISSUES OF HUMAN RIGHTS

Donnelly, Jack. *International Human Rights*. 4th ed. Boulder, CO: Westview Press, 2012.

Korey, William. *NGOs and the Universal Declaration of Human Rights*. New York: St. Martin's Press, 1998.

Lauren, Paul Gordon. *The Evolution of International Human Rights: Visions Seen*. Philadelphia: University of Philadelphia Press, 1998.

Robertson, A. H. and J. G. Merrills. *Human Rights in the World*. 4th ed. London: Manchester University Press, 1986.

BACKGROUND TEXTS ON THE UN, SPECIFIC POLICY MAKERS, AND THE INTERNATIONAL COMMUNITY

Boutros-Ghali, Boutros. *Unvanquished: A US-UN Saga*. New York: Random House, 1999.

Burgerman, Susan. *Moral Victories: How Activists Provoke Multilateral Action*. Ithaca, NY: Cornell University Press, 2001.

Kennedy, Paul. *The Parliament of Man: The Past, Present and Future of the United Nations*. New York: Vintage, 2007.

Lebor, Adam. *Complicity with Evil: The United Nations in the Age of Modern Genocide*. New Haven, CT: Yale University Press, 2008.

Meisler, Stanley. *Kofi Annan: A Man of Peace in a World of War*. Hoboken, NJ: Wiley, 2008.

Meisler, Stanley. *United Nations: The First Fifty Years*. New York: Atlantic Monthly Press, 1995.

Mills, Nicolaus and Kira Brunner, eds. *The New Killing Fields: Massacre and the Politics of Intervention*. New York: Basic Books, 2002.

Moore, Jonathan, ed. *Hard Choices: Moral Dilemmas in Humanitarian Intervention*. Lanham, MD: Rowman & Littlefield, 1998.

Power, Samantha. *"A Problem from Hell": America and the Age of Genocide*. New York: Basic Books, 2002.

Shawcross, William. *Deliver Us from Evil: Peacekeepers, Warlords and a World of Endless Conflict*. New York: Simon & Schuster, 2000.

Storey, Andy. "Structural Adjustment, State Power and Genocide: The World Bank and Rwanda." *Review of African Political Economy* 29 (2001): 365–85.

Traub, James. *The Best Intentions: Kofi Annan and the UN in the Era of American World Power*. New York: Picador, 2007.

Wheeler, Nicholas. *Saving Strangers: Humanitarian Intervention in International Society*. Oxford: Oxford University Press, 2000.

NOTES

Notes from Part Two: Historical Background

1. Jan Vansina, *Antecedents to Modern Rwanda: The Nyiginya Kingdom* (Madison: University of Wisconsin Press, 2004), pp. 35, 133–9.

2. Ibid., 136.

3. Mahmood Mamdani, *When Victims Become Killers: Colonialism, Nationalism, and the Genocide in Rwanda* (Princeton, NJ: Princeton University Press, 2001), chap. 3. The quotes are from pp. 87–88. See also Lee Ann Fujii, *Killing Neighbors: Webs of Violence in Rwanda*, (Ithaca: Cornell University Press, 2011), chap. 2.

4. Ibid., 86.

5. Catharine Newbury, *The Cohesion of Oppression: Clientship and Ethnicity in Rwanda, 1860–1960* (New York: Columbia University Press, 1988), chap. 4.

6. Alison Des Forges, *Defeat Is the Only Bad News: Rwanda under Musinga, 1896–1931* (Madison: University of Wisconsin Press, 2011), chap. 9.

7. Timothy Longman, *Christianity and Genocide in Rwanda* (New York: Cambridge University Press, 2011).

8. You can find the French version of this document at http://jkanya.free.fr/manifestebahutu240357.pdf, accessed 15 February 2018. For a good discussion, see Scott Strauss, *Making and Unmaking Nations: War, Leadership, and Genocide in Modern Africa* (Ithaca, NY: Cornell University Press, 2015), 277–281.

9. Human Rights Watch estimated up to 20,000 in its report "Arming Rwanda: The Arms Trade and Human Rights Abuses in the Rwanda" in *Human Rights Watch Arms Project*, Vol. 6. No. 1. (January 1994), p. 8. https://www.hrw.org/sites/default/files/reports/RWANDA941.PDF, accessed 16 February 2018.

10. Alison Des Forges, "Leave None to Tell the Story," (Human Rights Watch, 1999), https://www.hrw.org/reports/1999/rwanda/Geno1-3-09.htm#P250_110826, accessed 15 February 2018. See also Marie-Eve Desrosiers and Susan Thomson, "Rhetorical Legacies of Leadership: Projections of 'Benevolent Leadership' in Pre- and Post-Genocide Rwanda," *Journal of Modern African Studies*, 49 (2011): 429–453.

11. Gerard Prunier, *The Rwanda Crisis: History of a Genocide* (New York: Columbia University Press, 1995), p. 75.

12. André Guichaoua, *From War to Genocide: Criminal Politics in Rwanda, 1990-1994* (Madison: University of Wisconsin Press, 2015), pp. 23–30.

13. Willa Friedman, "The Economics of Genocide in Rwanda," in Charles H. Anderton and Jurgen Brauer, *Economic Aspects of Genocides, Mass Atrocities, and Their Prevention* (New York: Oxford University Press, 2016), pp. 340–41. See also Catherine Andre and Jean-Philippe Platteau, "Land Relations under Unbearable Stress: Rwanda Caught in the Malthusian Trap" *Journal of Economic Behavior & Organization* 34, no. 1(1998): 1–47.

14. Mamdani, *When Victims Become Killers,* p. 146.

15. Friedman, "The Economics of Genocide in Rwanda."

16. The statistics in this and the following paragraph are from Mamdani, p. 148.

17. See Daniela Kroslak, *The Role of France in the Rwandan Genocide* (Bloomington, IN: Indiana University

Press: 2007). The quote comes from Alan Riding, "France Ties African Aid to Democracy," *New York Times*, June 22, 1990, found at http://www.nytimes.com/1990/06/22/world/france-ties-africa-aid-to-democracy.html.

18. Prunier, *The Rwanda Crisis*, pp. 98–99.

19. Roméo Dallaire, *Shake Hands with the Devil* (New York: Carroll & Graf, 2003), p. 79ff.

20. Herman Salton, *Dangerous Diplomacy: Bureaucracy, Power Politics, and the Role of the UN Secretariat in Rwanda* (New York: Oxford University Press, 2017), chap. 3.

21. See Marie-Eve Desrosiers, "Rethinking Political Rhetoric and Authority during Rwanda's First and Second Republics" *Africa* 84, no. 2 (May 2014): 199–225; and Catherine Newbury and David Newbury, "A Catholic Mass in Kigali: Contested Views of the Genocide and Ethnicity in Rwanda," *Canadian Journal of African Studies / Revue Canadienne des Études Africaines* 33 (1999): 292–328.

22. See René Marchand, "The Burundi Massacre," in Samuel Totten and William Parsons, eds., *Century of Genocide*, 2nd ed. (New York: Routledge, 2004), pp. 321–338.

23. Marchand has emphasized this in a variety of works. In addition, see the brief but persuasive discussion in Guichaoua, pp. 6–12.

24. Libraries have shelf after shelf of books discussing the history of the United Nations. I've relied heavily on two of these: Paul Kennedy, *The Parliament of Man: The Past, Present, and Future of the UN* (New York: Vintage Books, 2006), and Mark Mazower, *Governing the World: The History of an Idea, 1815 to the Present* (New York: Penguin Books, 2012). You can find suggestions for other sources which address the contemporary history of the UN in the bibliography at the end of this game book.

25. For a thoughtful alternative explanation, see Adam Tooze, *The Deluge: The Great War, America and the Remaking of the Global Order, 1916–1931* (New York: Penguin, 2014).

26. Quoted in Kennedy, *The Parliament of Man*, p. 36.

27. See Raphael Lemkin and Donna-Lee Frieze, *Totally Unofficial: The Autobiography of Raphael Lemkin* (New Haven, CT: Yale University Press, 2013); and John Cooper, *Raphael Lemkin and the Struggle for the Genocide Convention* (New York: Palgrave Macmillan, 2008).

28. Kennedy, *The Parliament of Man*, pp. 52–54.

29. Francis Fukuyama, "The End of History?," *National Interest* (Summer 1989), pp. 3–18.

30. Michael Barnett, *Eyewitness to a Genocide: The United Nations and Rwanda* (Ithaca, NY: Cornell University Press, 2003), p. 26.

31. Lynn Hunt, *Inventing Human Rights* (New York: Norton, 2008); Samuel Moyn, *The Last Utopia: Human Rights in History* (Cambridge, MA: Belknap Press, 2012); and Paul Gordon Lauren, *The Evolution of International Human Rights: Visions Seen* (Philadelphia: University of Pennsylvania Press, 2011).

32. Mazower, *Governing the World*, pp. 381–82. See also chap. 1 in Barnett's excellent account: *Eyewitness to a Genocide.*

33. Most obviously in his report "An Agenda for Peace" (1992). See p. 118 of this game book.

34. For this and the following paragraph, see Salton, *Dangerous Diplomacy*, especially chaps. 1, 2, and 6.

35. Much of the following section is drawn from Barnett, *Eyewitness to a Genocide*, pp. 34–39.

36. See especially Robert Donia, *Radovan Karadzic, Architect of the Bosnian Genocide* (New York: Cambridge University Press, 2014).

37. Ed Vulliamy, *Seasons in Hell: Understanding Bosnia's War* (New York: St. Martin's, 1994); Roy Guttman, *A Witness to Genocide* (New York: Lisa Drew Books, 1993); and especially two books by Janine di Giovanni, *The Quick and the Dead: Under Siege in*

Sarajevo (London: Phoenix House, 1994) and *Madness Visible: A Memoir of War* (New York: Vintage, 2005).

38. For a compact but thorough institutional history (although it reads pretty slowly), see the UN report titled United Nations Protective Force, located at https://peacekeeping.un.org/mission /past/unprof_b.htm. For a more general history of the conflict in the former Yugoslavia, see the relevant chapter in William Hitchcock, *The Struggle for Europe: The Turbulent History of a Divided Continent, 1945 to the Present* (New York: Anchor, 2004); for a more personal story, see Chuck Sudetic, *Blood and Vengeance: One Family's Story of War in Bosnia* (New York: Norton, 1998).

39. See Adam Jones, ed., *Gender and Genocide* (Nashville, TN: Vanderbilt University Press, 2014); and the essays in Amy Randall's outstanding collection *Genocide and Gender in the Twentieth Century: A Comparative Survey* (New York: Bloomsbury, 2015).

40. For more, see James Waller, *Confronting Evil: Engaging Our Responsibility to Prevent Genocide* (New York: Oxford University Press, 2016), chaps. 1-3.

41. See Gary Jonathon Bass, *Stay the Hands of Vengeance: The Politics of War Crimes Tribunals* (Princeton, NJ: Princeton University Press, 2001).

ACKNOWLEDGMENTS

It is a mark of the nature of the communities of both Newman and Reacting that I cannot possibly thank everyone who has given me feedback, offered suggestions, or simply listened to me drone on and on about Rwanda over the years since I began designing this game. Here I want to say a special thank you to some of those who have been most important in making the game better.

In Reacting, thanks go out especially to Jeff Hyson, who has been the very model of what a development editor should be; to Nick Proctor, who read an early draft of the game and has provided support and feedback ever since; to Abby Perkiss and Becca Livingstone, for allowing me to sidetrack discussions about the games we were supposed to be designing to talk about Rwanda instead; to all the people who play-tested the game at the GDC in 2012 and at Barnard in 2014; and to Mark Carnes, who somehow managed to turn a rejection letter into encouragement in the value of the project. As usual, Dana Johnson, Maddie Provo, and Jenn Worth did the behind the scenes work to make the game widely available to those who wanted to play it on their campuses.

At Newman, thanks to former Provost Mike Austin, who played the first version of this game and provided encouragement and support throughout the process; to Cheryl Golden and David Shubert, who listened patiently while I turned every hallway encounter into a chance to tell another story about Rwanda; and to the Professional Development Committee, which approved request after request to attend conferences that advanced the game. Audrey Curtis Hane agreed to let me hijack our learning community to play-test the game year after year. In particular, I want to thank Steve Hammersky and Jeanette Parker, who filled countless Interlibrary loan requests over the years. Tiffany Perkins and Emily Kurtz uncovered countless errors in grammar and style during repeated readings of the text. Most of all, I want to thank the hundreds of students who played the game in my classes and gave me useful feedback about the process (albeit at the cost of pizza and BBQ). All of these comments were valuable. It should not diminish others' contribution to single out Monica Hill, Jaimie (Dungan) Fager, Mark Greene, Katie (Hamlin) Kissling, Alaina Garrett, and Emily Simon as having provided particularly useful suggestions.

Outside of Newman, I've benefited from the careful comments of two outstanding Rwanda specialists: Susan Thomson and Timothy Longman. And I've been thrilled to work with Justin Cahill and Rachel Taylor at Norton. I couldn't have asked for better editors.

Finally, my wife and children have been the center of my personal community. They have tolerated my physical absence from softball games, choir concerts, and family dinners and my even more egregious mental absence throughout the process of designing this game. They did so gladly, knowing how important teaching about human rights is to me. I trust they know that they are even more important.